KT-511-415

Microwave
ENTERTAINING

Compiled and Edited by Judith Ferguson
Recipes Tested and Prepared by Jacqueline Bellefontaine
Photographed by Peter Barry
Designed by Philip Clucas
Produced by David Gibbon, Gerald Hughes and Ted Smart

CLB 1987

Filmsetting by Focus Photoset Ltd., London, England.
Printed and bound in Barcelona, Spain by Cronion, S.A.

Published 1987 by Crescent Books, distributed by Crown Publishers, Inc.
ISBN 0 517 65295 1
h g f e d c b a

The publishers wish to thank Samsung Electronics (UK) Ltd for the loan of microwave ovens, Corning Ltd for providing Pyrex and microwave cookware and Lakeland Plastics of Windermere, Cumbria for the supply of cookware and accessories.

Microwave ENTERTAINING

CRESCENT BOOKS
NEW YORK

Contents

INTRODUCTION

Giving a party is supposed to be fun. Frequently, however, the thought fills some people with terror. The remedy for this is advance planning and dependable equipment, and one appliance that can help enormously is the microwave oven. It comes to the rescue in so many ways, from speedy preparation of sauces to last minute reheating of vegetables. Use it in combination with your labor-saving appliances, such as food processors and blenders, and really make entertaining easy.

Advance preparation is one of the best ways of insuring against that last-minute panic, and the following points are worth considering:

- Be flexible with the menu. Plan ahead, but be prepared to make final decisions depending on what is available and looks best when you are in the shops.
- Buy ingredients that will keep a few days in advance. Buy fresh ingredients the day before the party.
- Make a timetable. Write down the order in which you need to prepare, cook, reheat and serve dishes.
- Prepare appetizers and desserts in advance and reheat in your microwave oven as necessary at the last minute. If one of the dishes can be served cold, so much the better.
- If the main course is to be accompanied by a sauce, choose one that can be made in advance, and then frozen and reheated successfully.
- Pre-cook main courses if they will not spoil with standing. In particular, poultry can be cooked and then reheated in a sauce, and meat can be browned in advance. One of the great advantages of the microwave is that it reheats without drying out the food.
- Pre-cook rice, potatoes and pasta. All of these reheat successfully in a microwave oven. Choose vegetables that can be parboiled and reheated, too.
- Reheat directly on serving dishes whenever possible, thus saving time and the chore of washing up. The microwave is perfect for this.
- If you forget to take cheese or butter out of the refrigerator, both can be softened by heating on a LOW or DEFROST setting for 15-20 seconds.

When planning your menu, keep color, texture and shape in mind when choosing the food for each course, so that you have an interesting and varied meal. Also keep in mind the style of each dish; for example, don't choose an informal appetizer to precede a very formal main course and dessert.

While you are unlikely to forget that white wine goes with fish and white meats and that red wine should be served with red meats, you may be surprised at how pleasant the combination of a light red wine and salmon can be. Even though chicken and veal are white meats, if they are served in a dark, rich sauce they need a red wine. Smoked fish or spicy food can present a problem, but a Hock or Alsace wine is a good choice when a white wine is necessary. If choosing a dessert wine confuses you, remember that Champagne is always delicious!

With a well-planned menu and a microwave oven in the kitchen, you will have more time to enjoy yourself with your guests. Entertaining will be more "entertaining".

All the recipes in this book were prepared in an oven with a 700 watt maximum output. For 500 watt ovens add 40 seconds for each minute stated in the recipe. For 600 watt ovens add 20 seconds for each minute stated in the recipe. If using a 650 watt oven only a slight increase in overall time is necessary.

DINNER PARTY MENUS
MENU 1

Garlic Vegetables

PREPARATION TIME: 15 minutes

MICROWAVE COOKING TIME: 11-14 minutes plus standing time

SERVES: 6 people

1 small head cauliflower, broken into small flowerets
4oz broccoli
2oz pea pods
½ red pepper, seeded and finely sliced
½ yellow pepper, seeded and finely sliced
4 green onions, thinly sliced on the diagonal

DRESSING
½ cup prepared mayonnaise
2 cloves garlic, crushed
1 tbsp chopped parsley and chives, mixed
Pinch salt and pepper

GARNISH
1 hard-boiled egg, finely chopped

Place the cauliflower flowerets in a casserole with 4 tbsps salted water. Cover and cook on HIGH for 6-8 minutes, cut the broccoli spears into flowerets the same size as the cauliflower and keep the stalks for other use or discard. Place in a casserole with 2 tbsps salted water and cover loosely. Cook on HIGH for 4-5 minutes. Top and tail the pea pods and add to the broccoli 1-2 minutes before the end of cooking time. Drain all the vegetables and combine with the sliced red and yellow pepper and the green onions. Mix all the dressing ingredients together and stir carefully into the vegetables. Place the vegetables on serving plates and heat through for 1 minute on HIGH. Top with the chopped hard-boiled egg before serving. Surround with lettuce leaves or shredded lettuce if desired. Serve with French bread or melba toast.

Involtini alla Romana

PREPARATION TIME: 30 minutes

MICROWAVE COOKING TIME: 15-19 minutes

SERVES: 6 people

6 veal escalopes (about 4-6oz each)
6 slices Parma ham
8oz garlic cheese
1 tbsp chopped fresh oregano or basil or ½ tbsp dried
Salt and pepper

SAUCE
14oz canned tomatoes
1 onion, roughly chopped
Salt and pepper
1 bay leaf
Pinch nutmeg
4 tbsps dry white wine
6 tomatoes, peeled, seeded and cut into thin strips
1 tbsp chopped parsley
Grated Parmesan cheese (optional)

Flatten the veal between 2 sheets of wax paper using a rolling pin or meat mallet. Place a slice of Parma ham on top of each veal escalope. Mix the cheese and the marjoram together and divide evenly among the veal escalopes. Place the cheese in the middle and roll the veal and ham around the cheese. Arrange in a circle in a dish and cook, uncovered, on HIGH for 8-10 minutes. Set aside while preparing the sauce. Combine all the ingredients except the chopped parsley, the tomato strips and cheese in a small, deep bowl. Cook on HIGH, uncovered, for 6-8 minutes or until the onion has softened and the sauce has reduced. Purée in a food processor or blender and sieve out the seeds. Arrange veal in a serving dish, pour over the sauce and sprinkle on the chopped parsley and the tomato strips. Reheat for 1 minute on HIGH before serving. Sprinkle with cheese, if desired. Serve with pasta or Italian rice.

Zabaglione

PREPARATION TIME: 25 minutes

MICROWAVE COOKING TIME: 3½ minutes

SERVES: 6 people

½ cup marsala or sweet sherry
6 egg yolks
3 tbsps sugar
2 tsps grated lemon rind

Menu 1: Zabaglione (top left), Involtini alla Romana (top right) and Garlic Vegetables (bottom).

4-6 large peaches, nectarines or apricots, peeled
Lemon juice

Microwave meringues, crushed

Peel the peaches or nectarines according to the recipe for Peches Melba. Crush 3 or 4 meringues coarsely or use ratafia biscuits. Place the meringues or biscuits in the bottom of each of 6 dessert glasses. Cut the fruit in half and remove the stones. Slice thinly, toss in lemon juice and divide the fruit among the glasses. To prepare the zabaglione pour the marsala into a glass measure and microwave on HIGH for 30-45 seconds. Whisk the egg yolks, sugar and lemon rind together in a large bowl and then gradually whisk in the hot liqueur. Microwave the mixture on LOW or DEFROST for 1½ minutes, remove and whisk well and then continue to cook on the same setting for a further 1½ minutes, whisking halfway through the cooking time. Whisk again briefly and then spoon the mixture on top of the fruit and meringues or biscuits. Sprinkle with grated nutmeg if desired.

MENU 2

Salmon Quenelles

PREPARATION TIME: 10-15 minutes

MICROWAVE COOKING TIME: 20-21 minutes

SERVES: 4 people

1lb salmon
1 bay leaf
1 slice onion
1 blade mace
½ cup water
3 slices bread, crusts removed
3 tbsps heavy cream
2 egg whites
Salt and pepper

SAUCE
½ cup butter
2 egg yolks
1 tbsp white wine vinegar
1 tbsp lemon juice
1 tbsp green peppercorns, drained and rinsed if packed in brine
2 tbsps heavy cream
Salt and pepper

Skin the salmon and remove any bones. Place the skin with the bones, bay leaf, onion slice, blade mace and water in a bowl. Cook, uncovered, on HIGH 2-3 minutes or until boiling. Reduce the setting and cook for 10 minutes on LOW. Strain the liquid and make up to 6 tbsps with water if necessary. If the liquid exceeds 6 tbsps, continue cooking on HIGH until reduced. Cut up the fish and purée in a food processor with the bread, egg whites and fish cooking liquid. Blend in the cream by hand and season with salt and pepper. Pour 2 cups of hot water into a large, shallow dish. Cook on HIGH for 2-3 minutes or until very hot or boiling. Divide the fish mixture into equal portions and shape into ovals using 2 spoons. Place spaced well apart into the hot water and cover the dish. Cook on HIGH for 6 minutes, repositioning the fish quenelles halfway through cooking. Leave to stand while preparing the sauce. Melt the butter for 1½ minutes on HIGH and beat the egg yolks with the remaining ingredients. Whisk the egg yolks into the hot butter and cook on MEDIUM for 1 minute, stirring after 15 seconds. Do not allow the sauce to boil. If the sauce begins to curdle, place the bowl in another bowl of iced water to stop the cooking. Continue cooking the sauce for the remaining 15 seconds or until thickened. Stir in the peppercorns and cream. Serve with the salmon quenelles.

Lemon Duckling

PREPARATION TIME: 30 minutes plus marinating time

MICROWAVE COOKING TIME: 30 minutes

SERVES: 6 people

6 duck breast fillets, about 6oz each

MARINADE
2 tbsps vegetable oil
Juice of 2 lemons
1 clove garlic, crushed
½ tsp ground coriander
Salt and pepper
1 tbsp chopped parsley
1 bay leaf

SAUCE
Zest of 4 lemons
2 lemons segmented
2 tsps cornstarch
1½ tbsps water
½ cup chicken stock
1 tbsp soy sauce
2 tsps honey
Pinch salt and pepper

Wipe the duck breasts with paper towels and then score the skin to make a diamond pattern. Combine the marinade ingredients in a shallow dish or plastic bag, add the duck and turn to coat well. Cover and leave in the refrigerator for 4 hours, turning occasionally. Drain and reserve the marinade, discarding the bay leaf. Heat a browning dish according to the manufacturer's directions. Place the duck breasts skin side down three at a time on the dish and cook on HIGH for 3 minutes. Turn over and cook for a further 10 minutes, rearranging the duck once or twice

Menu 2: Fig and Apricot Charlottes (top), Lemon Duckling (center) and Salmon Quenelles (bottom).

during cooking. Leave to stand for 5 minutes while cooking the second batch. If desired, the duck may be browned under a preheated broiler for 1-2 minutes for crisper skin. Mix cornstarch and water in a small, deep bowl. Add the reserved marinade and stock and cook on HIGH for 2 minutes, stirring once or twice. Add the lemon segments, zest, soy sauce and honey. Pour the sauce over the duck to serve and garnish with lemon slices and fresh coriander if desired. Serve with rice.

Fig and Apricot Charlottes

PREPARATION TIME: 25 minutes

MICROWAVE COOKING TIME: 1-2 minutes plus standing time

SERVES: 6 people

8oz dried figs
8oz dried apricots
½ cup brandy
1lb cream or curd cheese
½ cup thick natural yogurt
3 tbsps honey
Halved toasted almonds
½ cup heavy cream
Nutmeg

Place the figs and the apricots in a deep bowl with the brandy and heat for 30 seconds-1 minute on HIGH. Leave to stand, covered, 2-3 minutes. Drain off the brandy and reserve. Place a circle of wax paper in the bottom of 6 individual custard cups. Cut the figs in half and press them flat. Press the apricots to flatten slightly. Use the fruit to line the sides of the dishes, seed side of the fig inside. Soften the cream or curd cheese for 30 seconds- 1 minute on MEDIUM. Stir in the yogurt, honey and the reserved brandy. Spoon the mixture into the molds, pressing down firmly against the base and the fruit lining the sides. Fold any fruit ends over the cheese filling and chill or freeze. To serve from frozen, leave overnight in a refrigerator and then at room temperature for 1 hour before serving. Turn the charlottes out onto a serving plate and carefully pour cream around the base of each. Remove the paper circles from the top and decorate with toasted almonds. Sprinkle nutmeg on the cream.

MENU 3

Lima Beans, Scallops and Bacon

PREPARATION TIME: 25 minutes

MICROWAVE COOKING TIME: 17-20 minutes

SERVES: 6 people

1½ lbs shelled fresh or frozen lima beans
6 rashers bacon, rind and bones removed
12 scallops, roes attached if possible

DRESSING
4 tbsps oil
1 shallot, finely chopped
1½ tbsps white wine vinegar
2 tsps Dijon mustard
Pinch sugar
Salt and pepper
1 tsp chopped thyme, parsley or chervil

Combine the lima beans with 6-8 tbsps hot water in a casserole. Cover and cook on HIGH for 5-6 minutes. Leave to stand, covered, while preparing the remaining ingredients. Place the bacon on a microwave rack or between 2-3 layers of paper towels on a plate. Cook on HIGH for 4-5 minutes, turning over halfway through. Leave to stand and, when cool, crumble or chop coarsely. Place the scallops in a circle in a shallow dish or casserole and cover the top loosely. Cook on MEDIUM for 7-8 minutes or until just firm. In a medium size bowl, combine the oil and the shallot and cook for 1 minute on HIGH, or until the shallot is just softened. Leave to cool and combine with the remaining dressing ingredients. If the lima beans are old, peel off the outer skins. If they are young, tender beans the outer skin may be left on. Add the beans and the bacon to the dressing and set aside. Cut the scallops in half through the middle or cut the white muscles into quarters and leave the roes whole. Add to the lima beans and the bacon in the dressing and cover the bowl. Heat through on HIGH for 1 minute and serve immediately on a bed of lettuce, radicchio, curly endive or lambs lettuce (mache).

Chicken Veronique

PREPARATION TIME: 35 minutes

MICROWAVE COOKING TIME: 40-50 minutes

SERVES: 6 people

6 boned chicken breasts, skinned
1 cup white wine
1 bay leaf
6 black peppercorns
1 slice onion
2 tbsps butter or margarine
1½ tbsps flour
2 tsps chopped fresh tarragon or 1 tsp dried tarragon
Salt and pepper
1 cup light cream
6oz green seedless grapes
Salt and white pepper

Menu 3: Fruit Shortcake (top), Chicken Veronique (center) and Lima Beans, Scallops and Bacon (bottom).

ALMOND RICE PILAF
2 tbsps butter or margarine
½ cup sliced almonds
1 medium onion, finely chopped
Pinch saffron
1 cup long-grain rice
1½ cups hot chicken stock or water

Place the chicken in a casserole with the wine, bay leaf, peppercorns and onion slice. Cover with pierced plastic wrap and cook on HIGH for 20-25 minutes or until the juices from the chicken run clear. Melt the butter for the sauce for 30 seconds on HIGH and stir in the flour. Strain on the chicken cooking liquid and stir in gradually. Add salt, pepper and tarragon and cook on HIGH for 3-5 minutes, or until thickened. Stir in the cream, add the grapes and leave the sauce to stand, covered, while preparing the pilaf. Melt the butter or margarine in a large bowl or casserole and add the almonds. Cook on HIGH for 1-2 minutes or until the almonds begin to brown. Add the onion and cook a further 2 minutes to soften the onion and to brown the almonds. Add the saffron, rice and hot stock or water. Stir well and cover the bowl. Cook on HIGH for 13-14 minutes, stirring occasionally. Leave to stand for 10 minutes before serving. To serve, place 1 chicken breast on each serving dish, loosely cover and reheat for 1-2 minutes on HIGH. Reheat the sauce for 1 minute on HIGH and coat some over each chicken breast. Serve the rest of the sauce separately and place a portion of almond rice pilaf on each serving plate. Garnish each serving with mint leaves and small bunches of grapes if desired.

Fruit Shortcake

PREPARATION TIME: 35 minutes

MICROWAVE COOKING TIME: 9½ minutes

SERVES: 6 people

PASTRY
2 cups all-purpose flour
1 tbsp ground cinnamon
4 tbsps powdered sugar
½ cup plus 2 tbsps butter or margarine, softened

TOPPING
1 cup redcurrant jelly
1lb strawberries, raspberries or blackberries
½ cup whipped cream
Shelled pistachio nuts or angelica, washed and cut into small diamonds

Sift the flour, cinnamon and sugar together, rub in the butter until the mixture is like fine breadcrumbs or work in a food processor. Place a circle of wax paper in the bottom of a 9 inch round dish. Press in the mixture and smooth down firmly. Cook on LOW or DEFROST for 8 minutes. If brown spots form, cover them with small pieces of foil and continue cooking. The shortcake is done when a skewer inserted into the center of the cake comes out clean. Cool for at least 1 hour in the baking dish. Remove the shortcake and place on a serving plate. Melt the redcurrant jelly in a small bowl on HIGH for 1 minute. Stir and then push through a strainer into a clean bowl. Brush a thin layer of jelly to within ½ inch of the edge of the pastry and allow to set slightly. Arrange the fruit on top of the jelly. If the strawberries are large, cut in half and place cut side down on the jelly. Reheat the jelly 30 seconds on HIGH and stir. Brush the fruit with a thin layer of jelly, making sure the holes between the fruit are filled with jelly. Allow to set and cool completely. Pipe rosettes of cream around the outside edge of the fruit and decorate with nuts or angelica.

Menu 4: Petits Vacherins (top), Veal with Wild Mushrooms (center) and Jerusalem Artichoke Soup (bottom).

MENU 4

Jerusalem Artichoke Soup

PREPARATION TIME: 25 minutes

MICROWAVE COOKING TIME: 8-9 minutes

SERVES: 6 people

8oz Jerusalem artichokes, peeled and sliced
2 potatoes, peeled and sliced
3½ cups chicken or vegetable stock
Salt and pepper
2 tbsps butter (optional)
½ cup whipping cream

GARNISH
1 small jar red caviar
6 tbsps thick yogurt
2 tbsps chopped fresh chives

Place the artichokes and potatoes in a large, deep bowl. Cover the bowl loosely with plastic wrap and cook on HIGH for 6 minutes or until soft. Add the stock, salt and pepper and the butter if using. Cover and cook 8 minutes on HIGH or until the stock just comes to the boil. Allow to cool slightly and pour into a food processor or blender and purée until smooth. Add the cream and adjust the seasoning. Reheat for 2-3 minutes on HIGH before serving and garnish each serving with a spoonful of yogurt, ½ tsp red caviar and some chives.

Veal with Wild Mushrooms

PREPARATION TIME: 25 minutes

MICROWAVE COOKING TIME: 14-15 minutes

SERVES: 6 people

2lbs veal, cut in large chunks
12 oyster or other wild mushrooms
4 tbsps butter or margarine
4 tbsps Dijon mustard
4 tbsps honey
4 tbsps Worcestershire sauce

VEGETABLE ACCOMPANIMENT
8oz salsify, peeled and cut into 3 inch pieces
3 carrots, peeled and cut to the same size as the salsify
½ a celeriac root, peeled and cut into strips
1 tbsp chopped parsley
1 tbsp fresh rosemary leaves
4 tbsps heavy cream

Mix together the mustard, honey, Worcestershire sauce and veal. Heat a browning dish according to the manufacturer's directions and melt the butter. When foaming, add the veal in small batches, pressing down firmly on one side, turning over and pressing down again to seal both sides. Cook in 2 batches. Cook on HIGH for 5 minutes. Add the mushrooms and cook 1 minute on HIGH, cover and keep them warm. Combine the meat juices with all of the vegetables and toss well to coat. Add the herbs and salt and pepper and microwave, uncovered, on HIGH for 2 minutes. Cover and continue cooking on HIGH for 6 minutes or until the salsify is tender. Stir in the cream. Reheat the veal for 1-2 minutes on HIGH and serve with the vegetables.

Petits Vacherins

PREPARATION TIME: 20 minutes

MICROWAVE COOKING TIME: 6 minutes

SERVES: 6 people

MERINGUES
1 egg white
4 cups powdered sugar
¼ cup finely chopped walnuts

SAUCE
12oz raspberries
Lemon juice to taste
Powdered sugar to taste

TOPPING
¾ cup whipping cream
Walnut halves
Reserved raspberries

To make the meringues, put the egg white into a bowl and whisk lightly with a fork. Add enough of the powdered sugar, sifted, to give a firm, pliable dough. It may not be necessary to add all the sugar. Keep the mixture covered while shaping the meringues. Put out a portion on a surface dusted with more powdered sugar and form a sausage about the thickness of a little finger. Cut into 1 inch pieces and place well apart on wax paper on a plate or microwave baking sheet. Cook for about 1 minute or until dry and crisp. Reserve 6-12 raspberries for decoration and put the rest into a food processor or blender with the lemon juice. Purée until smooth and add sugar to taste. Process again to mix the sugar and sieve the sauce to remove the seeds. Divide the sauce equally among 6 dessert plates and place a meringue on top of the sauce on each plate. Crush 6 of the meringues and set aside. Any remaining meringues may be frozen or stored in an airtight container. Whip the cream and pipe on top of each meringue. Sprinkle with the reserved crushed meringue and decorate with walnut halves and the reserved raspberries.

MENU 5

Oeufs en Croustade

PREPARATION TIME: 30 minutes

MICROWAVE COOKING TIME: 22-24 minutes

SERVES: 6 people

12 slices whole-wheat bread, crusts removed
6 tbsps butter

FILLING
4oz mushrooms, finely chopped
1 shallot, finely chopped
2 tsps butter or margarine
2 tsps flour
1 tbsp sherry
4 tbsps light cream
12 quail eggs

SAUCE
1 tbsp butter or margarine
1 tbsp flour
½ cup milk
1 tsp chopped parsley
1 small cap pimento, finely chopped
Salt and pepper
Paprika

Roll the slices of bread to flatten. Cut into 3 inch rounds with a pastry cutter. Melt the butter for 30 seconds on HIGH and brush over both sides of the bread rounds. Mold into small custard cups and cook for 3 minutes on HIGH until crisp. Remove from the custard cups and place on a serving plate. Combine the mushrooms, shallot and butter for the filling in a small bowl and heat for 2-3 minutes on HIGH, or until the shallot is soft and the mushrooms are cooked. Stir in the flour and add the sherry and cream. Season lightly with salt and pepper and cook on HIGH for 2-3 minutes or until thickened. Allow to cool slightly. Melt the butter for the sauce for 30 seconds on HIGH and stir in the flour. Beat in the milk gradually until smooth and cook for 2-3 minutes on HIGH, or until thickened. Add the parsley and the pimento, season lightly with salt and pepper and set aside, with plastic wrap pressed directly over the sauce. Bring water in a shallow dish to the boil with 1 tsp vinegar and a pinch of salt. This should take about 8 minutes. Carefully break each quail egg onto a saucer and gently lower the egg into the water. Return to the oven and cook on HIGH for 30 seconds-1 minute or until nearly set. Leave to stand for 1-2 minutes to complete cooking. Eggs may be cooked in advance and kept in cold water. Place the mushroom mixture in the bottom of each tartlet shell. Drain the quail eggs and place 1 egg in each tartlet. Spoon over the sauce and dust lightly with paprika. Arrange the tartlets in a circle on a serving dish and heat through for 1-2 minutes on MEDIUM. Serve immediately.

Quail with Garlic and Green Olives

PREPARATION TIME: 30 minutes

MICROWAVE COOKING TIME: 23-34 minutes

SERVES: 6 people

6 quail
4 tbsps butter or margarine
6 cloves garlic
1 cup brown stock
½ cup dry white wine
1½ tbsps cornstarch
½ tsp thyme
1 tbsp chopped parsley
Salt and pepper
18 large green olives, pitted and quartered
1 tsp Dijon mustard
Salt and pepper

POMMES PAILLASSON
4 tbsps butter or margarine
1lb potatoes, peeled and coarsely grated
Salt and pepper

First prepare the potatoes. Melt the butter in a round, glass dish for 1½ minutes on HIGH. Layer in the grated potatoes, pressing down well and seasoning in between each layer. Loosely cover the dish with plastic wrap and cook on HIGH for 10-15 minutes. Set aside while preparing the quail. Heat a browning dish according to the manufacturer's directions. Melt the butter and when foaming brown the quail, 2 at a time, on HIGH for 2-3 minutes. Combine all the remaining ingredients except the olives in a casserole dish and add the quail and the juices from the browning dish. Cover and cook on HIGH for a further 6-8 minutes. Stir the sauce occasionally while the quail are cooking. To serve, turn out the potatoes onto a heatproof serving dish and brown the top under a preheated broiler. Remove the quail from the sauce and trim them if necessary. Arrange the quail on top of the potato cake, cover and keep warm. Purée the sauce in a food processor or blender until the garlic is completely broken down. Sieve if desired and add the olives. Season with salt and pepper and reheat the sauce on HIGH for 1-2 minutes. Spoon some of the sauce over the quail to serve and serve the rest of the sauce separately. Serve with a green vegetable or carrots in parsley butter.

Chocolate Orange Mousse

PREPARATION TIME: 20 minutes

MICROWAVE COOKING TIME: 4-5 minutes

SERVES: 6 people

6oz semi-sweet chocolate
1 cup heavy cream
1 egg
Grated rind of half an orange
2 tsps orange juice

DECORATION
Orange rind cut into thin strips
½ cup heavy cream, whipped

Chop the chocolate into small pieces and combine with the cream. Heat

Menu 5: Oeufs en Croustade (below), Quail with Garlic and Green Olives (bottom) and Chocolate Orange Mousse (far right).

on HIGH for 2-3 minutes, stirring frequently until the chocolate has melted and the mixture is smooth. Beat the egg with the orange rind and juice and gradually beat in the chocolate mixture. Pour into 6 individual dessert dishes and heat for 1 minute on HIGH to thicken. Chill until set. To serve, whip the remaining cream and pipe 1 rosette on top of each serving dish. Place the strips of orange rind in a small bowl with 4 tbsps water and heat for 1 minute on HIGH to soften. Drain and rinse under cold water and pat dry. Sprinkle on top of the mousse to serve.

MENU 6

Avocado and Chicken Livers

PREPARATION TIME: 25 minutes

MICROWAVE COOKING TIME: 4½-5½ minutes

SERVES: 6 people

2 ripe avocados
8oz chicken livers
2 tbsps butter or margarine
1 shallot, finely chopped
1 tbsp sherry
4-6 tomatoes, peeled, seeded and thinly sliced

DRESSING
8 tbsps oil
Juice of 1 small lemon
2 tsps chopped fresh herbs
Pinch sugar
Salt and pepper
1 head curly endive

Heat a browning dish according to the manufacturer's instructions. Pick over the chicken livers and trim away any discolored parts. Melt the butter in the browning dish and add the chicken livers, tossing to coat well. Add the shallot and cook on HIGH for 4-5 minutes, or until the shallot is softened and the livers are just barely pink inside. Pour over the sherry and set aside. Cut the avocados in half and remove the stones. Peel and cut each avocado half into thin slices. Combine all the dressing ingredients and mix with the tomatoes. Arrange a bed of curly endive on each serving plate and place the avocados on top so that the slices form a fan. Spoon over the dressing. Slice the chicken livers thinly and place a portion at the bottom of each avocado fan along with some tomato slices. Loosely cover the dishes and reheat for 30 seconds on HIGH before serving.

Monkfish Medallions Paprika

PREPARATION TIME: 25 minutes

MICROWAVE COOKING TIME: 16-19 minutes

SERVES: 6 people

1lb monkfish tails, skinned and cut into ½ inch slices
6 tbsps white wine
1 red pepper, seeded and sliced
½ cup heavy cream
1 tbsp paprika
1 tbsp cornstarch
Salt and pepper
8oz fresh pasta
2 cups boiling water
1 tbsp oil
Pinch salt

Place the sliced monkfish and the wine in a shallow dish and cover loosely with plastic wrap. Cook on HIGH for 4 minutes. Place the red pepper in a deep bowl, cover loosely and cook on HIGH for 1-2 minutes to soften. Add the heavy cream and paprika and cook on HIGH for 2-3 minutes. Mix the cornstarch with the cooking liquid from the fish and add the cream and pepper. Add a pinch of salt and pepper to taste and cook on HIGH for a further 2-3 minutes or until thickened. Cover and set aside while preparing the pasta. Pour the boiling water into a deep bowl, add a pinch of salt and the pasta. Loosely cover and cook on HIGH for 6 minutes. Leave to stand for 3 minutes before draining. Place the pasta in a serving dish and arrange the monkfish slices on top. Pour over the sauce to serve. If necessary, reheat on HIGH for 1-2 minutes.

Oeufs à la Neige

PREPARATION TIME: 25 minutes

MICROWAVE COOKING TIME: 23-26 minutes

SERVES: 6 people

MERINGUE
2 egg whites
3 tbsps sugar
2 drops vanilla extract

ORANGE CUSTARD
1½ cups milk
Grated rind of ½ an orange
1 tbsp sugar
4 egg yolks
½ tsp cornstarch

CARAMEL TOPPING
6 tbsps sugar
6 tbsps water

Menu 6: Oeufs à la Neige (top), Monkfish Medallions Paprika (center) and Avocado and Chicken Livers (bottom).

To make the meringues, whisk the egg whites until stiff but not dry. Add the sugar gradually, whisking continuously until the meringue is stiff, smooth and shiny. Fill a large, shallow dish with hot water. Shape the meringue with 2 damp tablespoons into egg shapes and slide them carefully onto the hot water. Cook on LOW or DEFROST for 2-3 minutes. Turn the meringues over and cook again on LOW or DEFROST for a further 2-3 minutes. Heat the milk and the orange rind for the custard on HIGH for 2 minutes. Beat the sugar, egg yolks and cornstarch until light, and gradually pour on the milk, beating constantly. Cook the custard on LOW or DEFROST for about 12 minutes, stirring every 30 seconds. Remove the custard when it coats the back of a spoon. Pour into a large serving dish or individual dishes and chill. Carefully float the meringues on top of the custard. To prepare the caramel topping, combine the sugar and water in a small, deep bowl and cook on HIGH for 5-6 minutes until golden. Do not allow the syrup to become too dark as it will continue to cook after it is removed from the oven. Dip the caramel bowl into another bowl of cold water to stop the cooking and to thicken the caramel slightly. Using a fork, drizzle the caramel over the meringues on top of the custard and allow it to set before serving.

MENU 7

Watercress Soup

PREPARATION TIME: 20 minutes

MICROWAVE COOKING TIME: 14-17 minutes

SERVES: 6 people

4 medium-sized potatoes, peeled and thinly sliced
1 small onion, finely chopped
2 tbsps butter or margarine
3½ cups vegetable or chicken stock
1 bay leaf
Salt and pepper
2 bunches watercress, well washed and thick stems removed
½ cup heavy cream
Nutmeg

GARNISH
Reserved small watercress leaves

Place the potatoes, onion and butter into a large, deep bowl and loosely cover with plastic wrap. Cook on HIGH for 4-6 minutes or until the potatoes and onions are beginning to soften. Pour on the stock and add the bay leaf, salt and pepper. Re-cover the bowl and cook a further 8 minutes on HIGH or until the stock just comes to the boil. Allow to cool slightly and pour into a food processor or blender. Reserve 6 small sprigs of watercress for garnish and roughly chop the rest. Place the watercress in the blender or food processor with the soup and purée until smooth. The soup should be lightly flecked with green. Add the cream to the soup and adjust the seasoning. Add a pinch of nutmeg and reheat on HIGH 2-3 minutes before serving. Garnish with the small watercress leaves.

Plié a l'Indienne

PREPARATION TIME: 25 minutes

MICROWAVE COOKING TIME: 9½ minutes

SERVES: 6 people

12 flounder fillets
1 bay leaf
1 slice onion
6 black peppercorns
1 cup water
2 tbsps butter or margarine
1½ tbsps flour
½-1 tbsp mild curry powder
1 tsp turmeric
Salt and pepper
4 tbsps light cream
1 small can pineapple pieces

GARNISH
Toasted almonds
Desiccated coconut

Place the fish in a shallow dish with the bay leaf, onion slice, peppercorns and water. Loosely cover with plastic wrap and cook on HIGH for 4 minutes. Leave to stand while preparing the sauce. Melt the butter for 30 seconds on HIGH and stir in the flour. Strain on the fish cooking liquid and add the curry powder, turmeric and salt and pepper. Cook on HIGH for 5 minutes. Stir in the cream and drained pineapple, cover and set aside. Place the fish in a serving dish or on individual plates and coat with the sauce. Sprinkle with toasted almonds and desiccated coconut. Serve with rice.

Almond Float with Fresh Fruit

PREPARATION TIME: 25 minutes

MICROWAVE COOKING TIME: 13-15 minutes

SERVES: 6 people

1 tbsp gelatine
4 tbsps cold water
½ cup milk
1 tbsp sugar
½ tsp almond extract
Few drops red food coloring (optional)

Menu 7: Almond Float with Fresh Fruit (top), Plié a l'Indienne (center) and Watercress Soup (bottom).

Assortment of fruits such as lychees, peeled, kiwi fruit, peeled and sliced, star fruit, thinly sliced, kumquats, thinly sliced, papayas, peeled, seeded and thinly sliced or cut into cubes, melon, peeled, seeded and thinly sliced or cut into cubes

SYRUP
½ cup sugar
1 cup water
Almond extract or amaretto (almond liqueur)

Sprinkle the gelatine over the water in a small bowl or cup and leave to soften for 5 minutes. Melt on HIGH for 15-20 seconds or until clear. Mix the milk with an equal amount of water and add the sugar. Heat for 2-3 minutes on HIGH to dissolve the sugar. Allow to cool and stir in the gelatine and the almond extract and coloring if using, and pour into a shallow, rectangular dish. Chill in the refrigerator until set. Meanwhile, prepare the syrup. Combine the water and sugar in a deep bowl and stir well. Cook on HIGH for 8-10 minutes or until the sugar is completely dissolved and the syrup is boiling. Do not allow the syrup to brown. Check carefully, it may be necessary to remove the syrup from the oven before the end of cooking time. Leave to cool completely and add the almond extract or amaretto. Chill the syrup completely and, when the almond float is set and the syrup is cold, prepare the fruit as directed. Cut the almond float into diamond shapes about 3 inches in length. Place 2 diamond shapes on each of 6 serving plates and arrange an assortment of fruit around them. Spoon over the syrup to serve.

MENU 8

Green Beans, Pâté and Mushrooms

PREPARATION TIME: 20 minutes

MICROWAVE COOKING TIME: 9½-11 minutes

SERVES: 6 people

1lb young green beans
8oz mushrooms
4oz firm pâté

DRESSING
4 tbsps oil
1 clove garlic, crushed
2 tsps chopped chives
1 tsp chopped parsley
1½ tsps white wine vinegar
Salt and pepper

Cook the green beans in 2 tbsps salted water for 6 minutes on HIGH. Stir occasionally and leave to stand for 1-2 minutes. The beans should still be crisp. While the beans are standing, combine the mushrooms with half of the measured oil from the dressing in a small bowl and cook on HIGH for 1-2 minutes or until just softened. Slice the pâté into thin strips or cut into small cubes. Combine the remaining dressing ingredients with the mushrooms and toss with the green beans. Add the pâté and mix carefully. Heat through on HIGH for 30 seconds-1 minute before serving. Pile the mixture onto serving plates lined with lettuce leaves if desired.

Sole d'Epinard

PREPARATION TIME: 30 minutes

MICROWAVE COOKING TIME: 14-17 minutes

SERVES: 6 people

FILLING
8oz fresh spinach, stems removed and well washed
Salt and pepper
Nutmeg
3 slices white bread, crusts removed and made into crumbs
1 egg white
2 tbsps heavy cream

6 double fillets of sole
4 tbsps dry white wine

SAUCE
2 tbsps butter
2 tbsps flour
1 cup milk
Juice and rind of 1 lemon
Salt and pepper

TOPPING
Parmesan cheese, grated
Dry breadcrumbs

GARNISH
Lemon slices

Cook the spinach for 4 minutes on HIGH in a roasting bag or casserole, well covered. Drain and chop in a food processor with the salt and pepper, nutmeg and breadcrumbs. Add the egg white and process once or twice to mix. Stir in the cream by hand. Spread evenly over the fish fillets and fold or roll up. Place fish in a dish in a circle with the wine and cover with plastic wrap. Cook on HIGH for 4-5 minutes. Melt the butter for 30 seconds on HIGH and add the flour. Strain in the cooking liquid from the fish, add the milk and beat well. Cook on HIGH 3-5 minutes until thickened. Add the lemon rind and juice, salt and pepper. Arrange the sole in a serving dish and pour over the sauce. Mix the Parmesan cheese and the breadcrumbs together and sprinkle over the top. Brown under a preheated broiler or cook a further 2

Menu 8: Tartelettes aux Fruits (top), Sole d'Epinard (center) and Green Beans, Pâté and Mushrooms (bottom).

minutes on HIGH. Garnish with lemon slices. Serve with boiled potatoes or rice.

Tartelettes aux Fruits

PREPARATION TIME: 40 minutes

MICROWAVE COOKING TIME: 5½-8 minutes

SERVES: 6 people

PASTRY
1 cup all-purpose flour
2 tbsps toasted ground hazelnuts or almonds
5 tbsps butter or margarine
2 tsps sugar
1 egg yolk

FILLING
1 cup milk
2 egg yolks
4 tbsps sugar
2 tbsps cornstarch
¼ tsp almond extract

TOPPING
Selection of fresh fruit such as white or black grapes, strawberries, satsumas, apricots, cherries or kiwi fruit

GLAZE
Apricot jam
Redcurrant jelly

Rub the fat and flour for the pastry together until the mixture resembles fine breadcrumbs. Add the sugar and nuts and stir in the egg yolk. Knead lightly, wrap in plastic wrap and chill in the refrigerator for 30 minutes. Alternatively, prepare the pastry in a food processor, taking care not to over-mix. Roll the pastry out thinly on a floured board and cut into 12 rounds about 2 inches in diameter. Use the pastry to line microwave muffin trays or small custard cups. Prick the bases with a fork and cook on HIGH for 3 minutes. Cook in two batches of 6. Allow the pastry to cool slightly in the baking dishes and then transfer to a wire rack to cool completely. To make the filling, heat the milk for 1-2 minutes on HIGH, or until boiling. Beat the egg yolks, sugar cornstarch and almond extract together until light. Gradually pour on the milk, beating well. Return to the microwave oven and cook on HIGH for 1-2 minutes, stirring every 15 seconds until thick and smooth. Place wax paper directly over the top of the filling to allow it to cool without forming a skin. When the filling is nearly cool, spoon in equal amounts into each pastry shell. Cut the grapes in half and remove the seeds. Place them cut side down on top of the filling or cut into quarters and arrange in attractive patterns. Arrange the other fruit as desired, making sure that all the pith is removed from the satsuma segments. Melt the apricot jam and the redcurrant jelly in two separate bowls for 30 seconds to 1 minute on HIGH. Sieve both and use the apricot jam for the light colored fruit and the redcurrant jelly for the red fruit. Brush the glazes on the fruit while the glaze is still warm. Allow the glaze to set before serving.

MENU 9

Pea Pods and Jumbo Shrimp

PREPARATION TIME: 25 minutes

MICROWAVE COOKING TIME: 3-4 minutes

SERVES: 6 people

8oz pea pods
6oz jumbo shrimp, cooked and shelled
2 green onions, shredded or thinly sliced

Menu 9: Marrons en Chemise (top left) Noisettes d'Agneau Maltaise (top right) and Pea Pods and Jumbo Shrimp (bottom).

4-6 water chestnuts, thinly sliced

DRESSING
4 tbsps oil
Dash sesame oil
1 tsp grated fresh ginger
½ clove garlic, crushed
Juice and grated rind of half a lemon
Salt and pepper

Top and tail the pea pods and place in a bowl or casserole with 2 tbsps salted water. Cover loosely and cook on HIGH for 1-2 minutes. Set aside while preparing the other ingredients. Slice the water chestnuts thinly and slice the jumbo shrimp in half through the middle. Heat the oil with the sesame oil, ginger and garlic on HIGH for 1 minute. Allow to cool and combine with the remaining dressing ingredients. Drain the pea pods and combine with the shrimp, water chestnuts and green onions. Mix with the dressing ingredients and place on serving dishes. Reheat through on HIGH for 1 minute before serving.

Noisettes d'Agneau Maltaise

PREPARATION TIME: 30 minutes

MICROWAVE COOKING TIME: 26-32 minutes

SERVES: 6 people

6 noisettes of lamb cut from the best end, about 1½ inch thick
Oil

SAUCE MALTAISE
2 egg yolks
½ cup butter
Salt and pepper
Grated rind of ½ a blood orange

POMMES DUCHESSE
1½ lbs potatoes, peeled and cut into even-sized pieces
Salt and pepper
2 tbsps butter
2-4 tbsps hot milk
1 large egg, beaten
Paprika

First prepare the potatoes. Place them in a large bowl with a pinch of salt and 4 tbsps water. Cover with pierced plastic wrap and cook on HIGH for 5-10 minutes. Leave to stand for 5 minutes. Mash until smooth and then beat in the butter and pepper. Beat in the hot milk until smooth. Allow to cool slightly and then beat in the egg, reserving about half. Mix very well and fill a pastry bag fitted with a rosette tube. Pipe swirls of potato onto a plate covered with wax paper. Chill thoroughly. Heat a browning dish according to the manufacturer's directions. Lightly oil the surface and cook the noisettes 2 or 3 at a time, pressing them down against the hot browning dish on both sides to seal. Cook the noisettes on HIGH for about 7 minutes. Cover and keep warm while preparing the sauce. Melt the butter for 2 minutes on HIGH in a large glass measure. Beat the egg yolks together with orange rind. Add a pinch of salt and white pepper and gradually beat into the hot butter. Cook on MEDIUM for 1 minute, whisking after 15 seconds and at 15 second intervals thereafter. If the sauce begins to curdle, dip the glass measure into a bowl of iced water to stop the cooking and whisk well. Continue cooking until the sauce thickens. Cover the sauce and set aside. To finish the potatoes, brush with additional beaten egg mixed with a pinch of salt and sprinkle lightly with paprika. Cook on HIGH for 3-4 minutes until piping hot. Brown under a preheated broiler if desired. Reheat the noisettes for 1-2 minutes on HIGH if necessary and place on a serving dish, removing the string around each.
Spoon over some of the sauce and garnish with the segmented orange if desired. Place a swirl of potato on each plate and serve immediately.

Marrons en Chemise

PREPARATION TIME: 30 minutes

MICROWAVE COOKING TIME: 5-7 minutes

SERVES: 6 people

WHITE CHOCOLATE MOUSSE
1 cup milk
4oz white chocolate, roughly chopped
2 egg yolks, 1 white reserved
2 tbsps sugar
3 tbsps water
1 tbsp gelatine
½ cup whipping cream

Approximately 1 cup crème de marron (sweetened chestnut spread)

DECORATION
2-3 squares semi-sweet chocolate

Heat the milk for 2-3 minutes on HIGH with the chopped white chocolate. Beat the egg yolks and the sugar together until light. Gradually pour on the milk, stirring constantly. Return to the oven and cook on HIGH for 2-3 minutes, stirring every 15 seconds until the mixture coats the back of a spoon. Allow to cool. Meanwhile, sprinkle the gelatine on top of the water in a small bowl. Allow to stand for 5-10 minutes to soften and then melt on HIGH for 20-30 seconds. Pour into the cooled custard and set the bowl in another bowl of iced water. Allow to cool completely and stir frequently to help the gelatine to set evenly. Meanwhile, whip the cream and the egg white and fold into the custard when the gelatine is nearly set. Spoon the crème de marron into the bottom of each of 6 small dessert dishes. Pour the white chocolate mousse on top to cover before the mousse sets completely. Chill in the refrigerator until firm. To decorate, melt the chocolate for 20-30 seconds on HIGH, stirring frequently. Put into a small pastry bag fitted with a writing tube. Pipe out a lacy design on top of the white chocolate mousse and let the chocolate set before serving. Mousse may be prepared and assembled the day before serving. Decorate with chocolate no more than 2 hours in advance.

MENU 10

Tomato Farcis

PREPARATION TIME: 25 minutes

MICROWAVE COOKING TIME: 9-12 minutes

SERVES: 6 people

6 large tomatoes, peeled

FILLING
6oz low fat soft cheese
3oz cooked ham, finely chopped
1 clove garlic, crushed
1 tbsp chopped parsley
2 tsps chopped fresh thyme or ½ tsp dried thyme

GARNISH
Whole chives

ACCOMPANIMENT
Hot butter toast or melba toast

To peel the tomatoes, place 4 cups water in a large bowl, cover with plastic wrap and microwave on HIGH for 8-11 minutes or until boiling. Place 2 of the tomatoes in the water and leave to stand for 1-1½ minutes. Remove the tomatoes to another bowl of cold water and bring the hot water back to the boil. Repeat with the remaining 4 tomatoes. The skin should peel off easily. On the rounded end of the tomato, cut a slice about ½ inch. Scoop out the pulp, sieve and set aside the juice. Combine the tomato juice with the filling ingredients and spoon into the tomatoes. Set the tops on at an angle and place the tomatoes in a circle on a plate. Heat on HIGH for 1 minute and place on individual serving plates. Garnish the plates with whole fresh chives and serve with the toast.

Scallops aux Herbes

PREPARATION TIME: 25 minutes

MICROWAVE COOKING TIME: 23-24 minutes plus standing time

SERVES: 6 people

18-24 scallops with roes attached
6 tbsps dry white wine
1 bay leaf

SAUCE
¾ cup heavy cream
3 tbsps chopped mixed herbs such as tarragon, chives, chervil or marjoram
Salt and pepper
Squeeze lemon juice

WILD RICE PILAF
½ cup long-grain rice
½ cup wild rice
½ cup chopped walnuts
Salt and pepper

Place the scallops in a shallow dish with the white wine and bay leaf. Cover and cook on MEDIUM for 3 minutes. Leave to stand while preparing the remaining ingredients. Boil the cream for 5 minutes on HIGH. Add 2 tbsps of the cooking liquid from the scallops and cook a further 2-3 minutes on HIGH. Stir in the herbs, salt, pepper and lemon juice. To cook the rice, place in a casserole with 2 cups boiling, salted water. Cook on HIGH for 12 minutes and leave to stand 5-10 minutes. Drain any water that is not absorbed and add the walnuts. Reheat on HIGH for 2 minutes. Add the scallops to the sauce and reheat on HIGH for 1 minute. Serve the scallops on a bed of rice.

Petites Galettes Normandes

PREPARATION TIME: 30 minutes

MICROWAVE COOKING TIME: 10-11 minutes plus standing time

SERVES: 6 people

PASTRY
1 cup all-purpose flour
1 tsp ground allspice
4 tbsps butter or margarine
2 tsps brown sugar
1 egg yolk

FILLING
1lb dessert apples, peeled, cored and sliced
½ tsp ground cinnamon
2 tbsps apricot jam
1 cup heavy cream, whipped

TO DECORATE
6 browned hazelnuts

To make the pastry, sift the flour with the sugar and the allspice and rub in the butter until the mixture resembles fine breadcrumbs. Add the egg yolk and mix to a soft dough. Knead lightly and wrap in plastic wrap and chill in the refrigerator for 30 minutes. Alternatively, make the pastry in a food processor. Roll the pastry out thinly and cut into 12 rounds, 6 at 3 inches and 6 at 2 inches diameter. Place the rounds on a plate or microwave baking sheet and cook on HIGH for 3 minutes. Cook the pastry in 2 batches. Allow to cool slightly on the dish or baking sheet and then transfer to a wire rack to cool. Combine the apples, cinnamon and apricot jam in a casserole, cover and cook on HIGH for 4-5 minutes. Leave to stand for 5 minutes, uncovered, and leave to cool. Place a large round of pastry on a serving plate and top with some of the apple filling. Whip the cream until soft peaks form and pipe or spoon on top of the apple. Place the smaller round of pastry on top of the cream and pipe a rosette on top. Decorate the rosette with a hazelnut and sprinkle lightly with powdered sugar if desired.

Overleaf: Menu 10 – Tomato Farcis (left), Scallops aux Herbes (center) and Petites Galettes Normandes (right).

MENU 11

Spinach Mousse with Tomato Tarragon Sauce

PREPARATION TIME: 25 minutes

MICROWAVE COOKING TIME: 18-22 minutes plus standing time

SERVES: 6 people

½ cup whipping cream
½ clove garlic, crushed
1lb fresh spinach, stems removed and leaves well washed
2 eggs
Salt and pepper
Grated nutmeg

SAUCE
14oz canned plum tomatoes
1 shallot, roughly chopped
3 sprigs fresh tarragon or 2 tsps dried tarragon leaves
Salt and pepper
Pinch sugar
2 tsps tomato paste
1 tbsp white wine or tarragon vinegar

GARNISH
3 tomatoes, peeled, seeded and cut into small dice

To prepare the spinach mousse, place the spinach in a roasting bag and tie loosely with string. Cook on HIGH for 4-5 minutes or until wilted. Leave to stand for 1-2 minutes and drain if necessary. Combine in a food processor with the garlic, eggs, salt, pepper and nutmeg. Blend until a smooth purée. Stir in the cream by hand. Grease 6 small custard cups lightly with butter and place a round of wax paper in the bottom. Divide the mixture between the custard cups and cook in a shallow dish of hot water to come halfway up the sides of the custard cups. Loosely cover the dish and cook on HIGH for 5-6 minutes. The mousses should feel firm when lightly pressed and should rise slightly in the dishes. Set aside while preparing the sauce. Combine all the sauce ingredients except the vinegar in a deep bowl and loosely cover. Cook on HIGH for 8-10 minutes, until boiling rapidly. Allow to stand for 3-5 minutes and sieve or purée in a food processor. Push through a strainer to remove the seeds and stir in the vinegar. Place an equal portion of the sauce on each of 6 serving dishes and turn out the spinach mousses on top. Reheat 1 minute on HIGH. Place a spoonful of the tomato dice on top of each mousse and serve immediately.

Beef Stroganoff

PREPARATION TIME: 25 minutes

MICROWAVE COOKING TIME: 14½ minutes

SERVES: 6 people

4 tbsps butter or margarine
2lbs rump or sirloin steak, trimmed and cut into thin strips
8oz mushrooms, sliced if large
1 clove garlic, crushed
2 tbsps flour
4 tbsps brown stock
4 tbsps brandy or sherry
Salt and pepper
½ cup sour cream or whole milk yogurt
4 tbsps snipped chives

Heat a browning dish according to the manufacturer's directions. Melt the butter and, when foaming, brown the meat in three or four batches. Pour the contents of the browning dish into a casserole and sprinkle over the flour. Gradually stir in the stock and the brandy or sherry. Add salt and pepper to taste and cook on HIGH for 4 minutes. Add the mushrooms and cook for a further 4 minutes, covered. Add salt and pepper to taste and stir in the chives. Gently stir in the sour cream and cook for 30 seconds on HIGH. Serve with noodles.

Kissel

PREPARATION TIME: 20 minutes

MICROWAVE COOKING TIME: 9-11 minutes

SERVES: 6 people

4oz blackcurrants, canned or frozen
4oz redcurrants, canned or frozen
4oz canned or frozen black cherries, pitted
4 tbsps sugar
4 tbsps water
Grated rind and juice of 1 orange
1 cinnamon stick
4oz raspberries, fresh or frozen
4oz strawberries, fresh or frozen
1 tbsp arrowroot or cornstarch mixed with 4 tbsps brandy

TOPPING
½ cup heavy cream, whipped
½ cup natural yogurt or sour cream
1 tbsp powdered sugar
Grated nutmeg

Place the blackcurrants, redcurrants and cherries in a deep bowl along with their juices. Add the sugar, water, grated rind and juice of the orange and cinnamon stick. Cover with pierced plastic wrap and cook on HIGH for 7-8 minutes or until boiling. Strain, reserving the syrup. Place the fruit in another bowl with the strawberries and raspberries. Mix the arrowroot or cornstarch with the brandy, add to the reserved syrup and cook, about 2-3 minutes on HIGH until thickened and clear. Remove the cinnamon stick and pour over the fruit. Stir well and leave to cool slightly. To serve, spoon the fruit mixture into glasses or dessert dishes. Whip the cream lightly and fold in the powdered sugar and sour cream or natural yogurt. Top each serving with some of the cream and sprinkle on nutmeg to serve.

Menu 11: Kissel (top), Beef Stroganoff (center) and Spinach Mousse with Tomato Tarragon Sauce (bottom).

MENU 12

Coquilles aux Poissons Fumé

PREPARATION TIME: 25 minutes

MICROWAVE COOKING TIME: 22-30 minutes

SERVES: 6 people

¾ lb smoked haddock fillets
¾ lb smoked cod fillets
½ cup dry white wine
1 bay leaf
3 parsley stalks

SAUCE
1 shallot, finely chopped
½ clove garlic, chopped
½ cup dry white wine
½ cup cooking liquid from the fish
2 tbsps butter or margarine
2 tbsps flour
Pinch turmeric
½ tsp dill seed
½ cup heavy cream
Squeeze lemon juice
Salt and pepper

GARNISH
Sprigs of fresh dill
2oz smoked salmon, cut into thin strips

Cut the fish into 1 inch pieces, place in a shallow casserole, pour over the wine and add the parsely and bay leaf. Loosely cover and cook on HIGH for 1-2 minutes. Leave to stand, covered, while preparing the remaining ingredients. For the sauce, put the shallots, garlic, wine, turmeric and dill seed into a small, deep bowl or glass measure. Cook on HIGH for 8-10 minutes, or until boiling. Allow to boil another 2-3 minutes to reduce slightly. Strain the liquid and reserve. Melt the butter in a small casserole for 30 seconds on HIGH and stir in the flour. Pour in the reduced wine mixture and strain on the required amount of fish cooking liquid. Stir well and cook on HIGH for 4-5 minutes, or until thickened. Pour the cream into a deep bowl or glass measure and cook on HIGH for 6-8 minutes to reduce. Pour into the sauce and blend well. Season with salt and pepper. Divide the haddock and cod among 6 shells or shell-shaped dishes. Pour over the sauce, loosely cover the dishes and reheat on HIGH for 1-2 minutes. Garnish the dishes with strips of smoked salmon and sprigs of fresh dill.

Lamb Poivrade

PREPARATION TIME: 35 minutes

MICROWAVE COOKING TIME: 26-30 minutes

SERVES: 6 people

4 best end necks of lamb

SAUCE
2 tbsps butter or margarine
2 tbsps flour
1 onion, finely chopped
1 clove garlic, crushed
1 cup rich brown stock
4 tbsps dry white wine
1 tsp tomato paste
1 bay leaf
1 sprig thyme
Salt
1 tbsp green peppercorns, slightly crushed (drained and rinsed if packed in brine)

POMMES DAUPHINOISE
4 tbsps butter or margarine
1 clove garlic, peeled
1lb potatoes, peeled and thinly sliced
½ cup light cream
1 egg, beaten
Salt and pepper
Grated nutmeg
½ cup grated Gruyère cheese

First prepare the potatoes. Melt the butter in a round dish or casserole with the garlic for 1½ minutes on HIGH. Remove the garlic clove and arrange the potatoes in neat layers, seasoning with salt, pepper and nutmeg in between each layer. Cover the dish with plastic wrap and cook on HIGH for 9 minutes. Remove the dish from the oven. Whisk the cream and the egg together and pour evenly over the potatoes, shaking the dish gently to allow it to seep down the sides to the bottom. Re-cover and cook on HIGH for 6 minutes more. Uncover the dish, sprinkle the cheese over the top and leave to stand while preparing the lamb. Trim away the bones and all the fat from each best end neck of lamb until only the eye of the meat remains. Slice into ½ inch thick slices. Heat a browning dish according to the manufacturer's directions and lightly grease with oil. Press the slices of lamb down firmly on one side and turn over and press again to seal both sides. Cook in several batches. Set aside, covered, while preparing the sauce. Put the remaining butter in the browning dish and add the onion and flour. Cook on HIGH for 3-4 minutes or until the onion and the flour are beginning to brown. Deglaze the browning dish with some of the stock and pour the contents into a casserole dish. Add the remaining stock, white wine, tomato paste, bay leaf and sprig of thyme. Season with salt and cook on HIGH 3-5 minutes or until thickened. If desired, a few drops of gravy browning may be added to make the sauce darker. Add the peppercorns and the lamb and stir well. Cover and cook on HIGH for 3 minutes to heat through and finish cooking the lamb. Reheat the potatoes for 1-2 minutes on HIGH. Brown under a preheated broiler and cut into even-sized portions. Serve with the Lamb Poivrade and lightly cooked pea pods.

Menu 12: Pêches Melba (top left), Pommes Dauphinoise (top right) Lamb Poivrade (center) and Coquilles aux Poissons Fumé (bottom).

Pêches Melba

PREPARATION TIME: 25 minutes

MICROWAVE COOKING TIME: 10-14 minutes

SERVES: 6 people

2 cups vanilla ice cream
6 ripe peaches
8oz raspberries, fresh or frozen
2 tsps lemon juice
Powdered sugar to taste
4 tbsps raspberry liqueur
Ground blanched almonds

Place the vanilla ice cream in a bowl and soften for 20-30 seconds on HIGH. Place in a pastry bag and quickly pipe the ice cream in swirls into 6 individual dishes, filling them halfway. Freeze the dishes until the ice cream is firm. Meanwhile, place 4 cups water in a large bowl. Cover with plastic wrap and heat on HIGH for 8-11 minutes or until boiling. Place 3 of the peaches in the water and allow to stand for 1-2 minutes. Remove the fruit to a bowl of cold water and then peel. Return the bowl to the oven and reboil the water. Repeat with the remaining 3 peaches. To prepare the sauce, combine the raspberries and lemon juice in a deep bowl and cook on HIGH for 2-3 minutes. Place in a food processor or liquidizer and purée until smooth. Add powdered sugar to taste and process once or twice to mix well. Strain out the seeds and push as much of the purée through the sieve as possible. Stir in the raspberry liqueur and set the sauce aside. Soften the ice cream at room temperature for 15 minutes. To serve, place a peach on top of the ice cream in each dish and spoon over some of the raspberry sauce. Sprinkle the top of the peaches with some of the blanched ground almonds. Serve the remaining sauce separately.

MENU 13

Consommé Valentine

PREPARATION TIME: 20 minutes

MICROWAVE COOKING TIME: 10-11 minutes

SERVES: 6 people

1 large carrot, thinly sliced
1-2 turnips, depending upon size, peeled and thinly sliced
1 tbsp chopped chervil or parsley
4 cups canned or freshly prepared chicken or beef consommé
4 tbsps sherry

Cut each slice of carrot and turnip into a heart shape with a small cookie cutter. Place the carrots and turnips in separate bowls with 1 tbsp water in each. Loosely cover the bowls with plastic wrap and cook on HIGH for 2-3 minutes. Leave to stand while reheating the consommé. Pour the consommé into a microwave proof soup tureen or individual bowls and add the sherry and chervil or parsley. Cover loosely and cook on HIGH for 8 minutes for the soup tureen or 2-3 minutes for individual bowls. Halfway through the reheating time, add the drained carrot and turnip hearts. Serve hot.

Poulet au Concombres

PREPARATION TIME: 30 minutes

MICROWAVE COOKING TIME: 20-28 minutes

SERVES: 6 people

6 chicken breasts, skinned and boned
1 cup chicken stock
1 small cucumber, seeded and cut into thin strips, but not peeled
2 tbsps butter or margarine
1½ tbsps flour
Salt and pepper
¾ cup light cream
2 tbsps chopped fresh dill or 1 tbsp dried dill weed

GARNISH
Whole sprigs of fresh dill

Place the chicken breasts in a dish in a circle and pour over the chicken stock. Cover with pierced plastic wrap and cook on HIGH for 15-20 minutes or until the juices from the chicken run clear. If desired, cut the chicken breasts into thin strips. Alternatively, leave whole if they have retained their shape. Melt the butter for 30 seconds on HIGH and stir in the flour. Strain on the cooking liquid from the chicken and add the cream. Season with salt and pepper and add the chopped dill. Cook on HIGH for 3-5 minutes, stirring occasionally until thickened. Place the chicken in a serving dish with the cucumber strips, loosely cover and reheat on HIGH for 2-3 minutes. Pour over the sauce to serve. Garnish with fresh dill.

Pavlova

PREPARATION TIME: 30 minutes

MICROWAVE COOKING TIME: 3 minutes

SERVES: 6 people

6 egg whites
1½ cups sugar
¼ tsp vanilla extract
2 tsps cornstarch
1 tsp white distilled vinegar
½ cup toasted sliced almonds

Menu 13: Pavlova (top), Consommé Valentine (center) and Poulet au Concombres (bottom).

FILLING
1 small pineapple, peeled, cored and cut into pieces or 8oz canned pineapple pieces, drained
2 kiwi fruit, peeled and sliced
1 passion fruit
4oz fresh strawberries (if available) or 2 oranges, peeled and segmented
1 cup whipping cream
Powdered sugar

Beat the egg whites until stiff peaks form. Add the sugar, a spoonful at a time, beating well in between each addition, until the meringue is stiff and glossy. Fold in the vanilla, vinegar and cornstarch. Spread the meringue in a circle on the plate or serving dish and make a deep well in the center. Do not spread to the edge of the plate. Sprinkle with the toasted almonds and cook on HIGH for 3 minutes. Allow to cool completely. Mix half the fruit with half the cream and fill the well in the center of the pavlova. Reserve the passion fruit for the top. Spoon or pipe the remaining cream into the center of the pavlova and decorate the top with the remaining fruit, scooping out the seeds and pulp from the passion fruit to drizzle on top as a sauce. Sprinkle lightly with powdered sugar and chill before serving.

MENU 14

Artichokes with Orange Mousseline Sauce

PREPARATION TIME: 30 minutes
MICROWAVE COOKING TIME: 17½-23 minutes
SERVES: 6 people

6 medium globe artichokes
½ cup salted water
2 tbsps lemon juice
1 bay leaf

SAUCE
½ cup butter
1 tbsp orange juice
1 tbsp lemon juice
2 egg yolks
1 tsp chopped tarragon
Salt and pepper
4 tbsps whipped cream

Wash the artichokes and trim off the stems and the lower leaves. Trim the pointed ends off all the leaves and place the artichokes in a large casserole or bowl with the salted water, lemon juice and bay leaf. Cook on HIGH for 15-20 minutes, turning the dish or re-arranging the artichokes twice during cooking. To test if the artichokes are cooked, pull one of the leaves from the bottom, it should come away easily. Drain the artichokes upside down on paper towels and leave to cool. To prepare the sauce, heat the butter in a glass measure for 2 minutes on HIGH. Beat the egg yolks and the orange and lemon juice together with salt and pepper and tarragon. Gradually whisk the egg yolks into the butter. Cook on MEDIUM for 1 minute, whisking well after 15 seconds. Do not allow the sauce to boil. If the sauce looks curdled, dip the glass measure into a bowl of iced water and whisk well. Continue heating until the sauce thickens. Allow to cool slightly and fold in the whipped cream. Carefully separate the center leaves on the artichoke and, using a teaspoon, remove the thistle-like choke from the inside. Reshape the artichoke and place 1 on each serving plate. Reheat on HIGH for 30 seconds-1 minute and serve with the mousseline sauce.

Stuffed Trout

PREPARATION TIME: 35 minutes
MICROWAVE COOKING TIME: 39-44 minutes
SERVES: 6 people

6 even-sized rainbow trout, boned

FILLING
6oz crab meat
1 tbsp snipped chives
1 package low fat soft cheese
5 slices bread, crusts removed made into crumbs
Cayenne pepper
Salt
6 tbsps butter
Juice of half a lemon
2 tbsps chopped parsley

GARNISH
Lemon slices

NEW POTATOES
1lb new potatoes, scrubbed but not peeled
1 cup water
Salt
3 tbsps butter or margarine

Ask the fishmonger to bone the trout. Mix the filling ingredients together and stuff each trout. Cover the heads and tails with foil and place the trout, three at a time, in a shallow dish. Cover with plastic wrap and cook 12 minutes on HIGH. Set the trout aside while cooking the remaining fish. In a deep bowl, microwave the butter for 2 minutes on HIGH until lightly brown. Add the lemon juice and parsley and set aside. To cook the potatoes, place them in a casserole dish with salt and water. Cover and cook on HIGH for 10-14 minutes. Drain and reheat with the butter 1-2 minutes. Leave to stand, covered. Reheat the fish for 2 minutes on HIGH and pour over the butter to serve. Garnish with lemon slices.

Menu 14: Artichokes with Orange Mousseline Sauce (top left), Flummery (top right) and Stuffed Trout (bottom).

Flummery

PREPARATION TIME: 30 minutes

MICROWAVE COOKING TIME: 9-10 minutes

SERVES: 6 people

2 tbsps butter or margarine
1 cup porridge oats
1 pint milk
2 tbsps cornstarch
1 tbsp gelatine
3 tbsps water
2-3 tbsps honey
3 tbsps Scotch or malt whiskey
½ cup heavy cream
4oz berries such as blackberries, blackcurrants, blueberries or strawberries

Melt the butter for the topping on HIGH for 30 seconds and stir in the oats. Cook for a further 3 minutes on HIGH, stirring occasionally, until the oats are evenly browned. Set aside. Mix the milk and the cornstarch together in a deep bowl and cook on HIGH for 5-6 minutes, stirring every minute until the mixture thickens. Allow to cool, covered with wax paper to prevent a skin from forming. Sprinkle the gelatine over the water and allow to soak for 5 minutes. Cook on HIGH for 15-20 seconds to dissolve. Stir the gelatine, honey and whiskey into the thickened milk mixture. Whip the cream until soft peaks form and fold into the mixture. Taste the berries and sweeten with more honey if desired. Place some of the berries in the bottom of a glass dessert dish and sprinkle over some of the topping. Spoon in flummery mixture and continue alternating with the oats, fruit and mixture for the 6 dishes. Finish with a layer of oats and a few pieces of fruit. Serve cold.

MENU 15

Cream of Smoked Salmon Soup

PREPARATION TIME: 15 minutes

MICROWAVE COOKING TIME: 11-14 minutes

SERVES: 6 people

¾ lb whitefish, skinned, boned and cut into 1 inch chunks
9oz smoked salmon, cut into 1 inch pieces, with 6 thin strips reserved for garnish
3 tbsps butter or margarine
3 tbsps flour
½ cup dry white wine
3½ cups milk
½ cup heavy cream
Freshly ground white pepper
1 tsp tomato paste (optional)

GARNISH
Sour cream
Chopped chives

Combine the whitefish and smoked salmon with the white wine in a large, deep bowl. Cover and cook on HIGH for 2-3 minutes. Leave to stand for 1-2 minutes before spooning into a food processor or blender. Add the milk and purée until smooth. Rinse out the bowl and melt the butter for 1 minute on HIGH. Stir in the flour and gradually pour in the milk and fish mixture. Heat for 3-5 minutes on HIGH, or until thickened. Add the pepper and the cream and reheat a further 5 minutes on HIGH. If the color of the soup is too pale, add 1 tsp tomato paste. Garnish with sour cream, chopped chives and the reserved strips of smoked salmon.

Fillet Steaks Rossini

PREPARATION TIME: 20 minutes

MICROWAVE COOKING TIME: 14-18 minutes

SERVES: 6 people

MADEIRA SAUCE
2 tbsps butter
2 tbsps flour
1 small onion, finely chopped
1 cup rich brown stock
4 tbsps Madeira or sherry
½ tsp tomato paste
1 bay leaf
Salt and pepper
Gravy browning (optional)

6 filet mignons
2 tbsps butter or margarine

GARNISH
3oz firm pâté
6 mushroom caps, fluted if desired

Heat a browning dish according to the manufacturer's directions and add the butter for the Madeira sauce. Add the onion and the flour and cook on HIGH, stirring frequently, until the flour and the onions brown lightly – this should take about 5 minutes. Deglaze the browning dish with some of the brown stock and spoon the contents into a deep bowl. Add the remaining stock and the bay leaf. Cook on HIGH for 3-5 minutes or until thickened. Strain into a clean bowl and discard the onions and bay leaf. Add the Madeira, tomato paste, salt and pepper and gravy browning, if using. Cover the sauce and set it aside. Clean the browning dish and reheat. Add the butter for the steaks and, when foaming, place three steaks on the browning dish and press down firmly. Turn over and press again to seal both sides. Cook the steaks on HIGH for 4 minutes. Repeat with the remaining steaks. Place all the steaks on individual serving dishes. Top each with a round, thin slice of pâté, cover well and keep warm. Add the mushrooms to the browning dish and cook for 1-2 minutes on HIGH, stirring occasionally. Place 1 mushroom on top of each slice of pâté and re-cover the meat. Reheat the Madeira sauce on HIGH for 1-2 minutes and spoon some over each steak. Serve the remaining sauce separately. Serve with an accompaniment of green beans cooked with thinly sliced red peppers.

Raspberry Sorbet in Chocolate Cups

PREPARATION TIME: 35 minutes

MICROWAVE COOKING TIME: 6 minutes

SERVES: 6 people

RASPBERRY SORBET
8oz fresh or frozen raspberries
¾ cup sugar
2 tbsps lemon juice
1 egg white, stiffly beaten

CHOCOLATE CUPS
3 squares semi-sweet chocolate
1½ tsps vegetable shortening

TO SERVE
6 tbsps raspberry liqueur
12 whole raspberries
Mint leaves

If using frozen raspberries, thaw on DEFROST for about 1-2 minutes. Purée the fruit in a food processor or blender and sieve to remove the seeds. Combine the sugar with ½ cup water in a deep bowl or glass measure. Heat on HIGH for 4 minutes, stirring every minute. Allow the syrup to cool and add the lemon juice. Stir in the fruit purée and pour the mixture into a freezer container. Freeze until the mixture is slushy, return to the food processor and beat until smooth. Return to the freezer and freeze again until almost solid. Take out the mixture and process again in the food processor or blender, adding the stiffly beaten egg white. Return to the freezer until firm. To make the chocolate cups, combine the chocolate in a small bowl with the vegetable shortening and cook on HIGH for 2-2½ minutes until melted. Stir frequently while melting. Use a double layer of cup cake liners and fill 6 cases with an equal amount of chocolate. Tilt case to coat the sides to within ¼ inch of the top. Continue to tilt to form a thick chocolate layer. Alternatively, brush on the chocolate with a pastry brush. Chill until set. Thirty minutes before serving, remove the sorbet from the freezer to allow it to soften. Alternatively, heat the container on HIGH for 20 seconds to soften. Carefully peel away the paper from the chocolate cups and place 1 on each serving plate. Fill with 1 scoop of sorbet and pour a spoonful of raspberry liqueur over the sorbet. Garnish with fresh raspberries and mint leaves.

Menu 15: Raspberry Sorbet in Chocolate Cups (top), Fillet Steaks Rossini (center) and Cream of Smoked Salmon Soup (bottom).

BRUNCH

Apricot Cheesecake

PREPARATION TIME: 40 minutes

MICROWAVE COOKING TIME: 12-17 minutes

SERVES: 8 people

BASE

1 cup all-purpose flour, sifted
Pinch salt
2 tbsps butter or margarine
2 tsps fresh yeast
2 tsps sugar
1 egg, separated

FILLING AND TOPPING

8oz cream or curd cheese
2 tbsps sugar
Grated rind of 1 lemon
4 tbsps light cream
1 egg, separated
1lb fresh or canned apricots, halved and stoned
Demerara sugar

Sift the flour and salt and rub in the butter by hand or with a food processor. Mix the yeast with 1 tbsp warm water and the sugar. Beat the egg yolk and add to the flour with the yeast. Mix together to form a smooth dough by hand or with a food processor and then knead for about 10 minutes, by hand on a lightly-floured surface. Roll the dough out to line a 9 inch round dish. Trim the edges and cover the dish with plastic wrap. Heat on HIGH for 15 seconds and then leave to rise for about 30 minutes or until a finger mark stays when the dough is lightly pressed. Cook on HIGH for 3-4 minutes, turning the dish occasionally. Leave to cool in the dish. To prepare the filling, mix the cheese, sugar, lemon rind, cream and the egg yolk together until smooth. Whisk both the egg whites until stiff but not dry and fold into the cheese mixture. Chop half of the apricots and arrange them over the dough base. Spoon the cheese mixture over the apricots and arrange the remaining apricot halves over the top of the cheese. Cook on HIGH for 4-5 minutes or until just beginning to set. Sprinkle with the demerara sugar and continue cooking for 5-8 minutes until the center is set. Turn the dish occasionally while the cheesecake is cooking. The top may be browned under a preheated broiler before serving if desired.

Red Fruit Compôte

PREPARATION TIME: 20 minutes

MICROWAVE COOKING TIME: 7-8 minutes

SERVES: 8 people

2lbs of the following fruits: cranberries; redcurrants, topped and tailed; cherries, fresh or canned, pitted; plums, halved and stoned; strawberries; raspberries.
½ cup sugar
2 tbsps cornstarch
½ cup orange juice

TOPPING

Natural yogurt
Ground cinnamon

Combine the cranberries, redcurrants and plums with sugar in a large, deep bowl. Cover and cook on HIGH for 3 minutes. If the cherries are fresh, add them with the cranberries, redcurrants and plums. If canned cherries are used, add them and their juice to the cooked fruit. Combine the cornstarch and the orange juice in a small, deep bowl or a glass measure. Strain on ½ cup of the cooked fruit juice and stir well. Cook on HIGH 4-5 minutes, or until thickened. Fold carefully into the cooked fruit and allow the mixture to cool. When completely cooled add the strawberries and raspberries and chill before serving. Serve topped with natural yogurt sprinkled with cinnamon.

Red Flannel Hash

PREPARATION TIME: 20 minutes

MICROWAVE COOKING TIME: 19-22 minutes

SERVES: 8 people

6 potatoes, peeled and cut into small dice
2lbs corned beef
1 onion, finely chopped
4 cooked beets, peeled and diced
Salt and pepper
2 tbsps Worcestershire sauce
Dash tabasco
3 tbsps butter or margarine
Chopped parsley

Place the potatoes in a large bowl with 6 tbsps water. Cover with plastic wrap and cook on HIGH for 5 minutes. Cut the corned beef roughly and drain the potatoes. Mix with the onions, beets and seasonings. Place the mixture into a shallow dish or

Facing page: Apricot Cheesecake (top) and Red Fruit Compôte (bottom).

individual dishes and dot the top with butter or margarine. Cook on HIGH for 9-12 minutes. Leave to stand for 5 minutes before serving sprinkled with chopped parsley. Poached eggs may be served on top.

Sherried Kidneys and Mushrooms

PREPARATION TIME: 15 minutes

MICROWAVE COOKING TIME: 18 minutes

SERVES: 8 people

4-6 veal kidneys, cored and cut into small pieces
8oz even-sized mushrooms, left whole
1 onion, finely chopped
3 tbsps butter or margarine
3 tbsps flour
1 clove garlic, crushed
1 cup brown stock
½ cup dry sherry
¼ tsp thyme
1 tbsp tomato paste
3 tbsps heavy cream
Chopped parsley
Toast

Heat a browning dish according to the manufacturer's directions. Melt 1 tbsp of the butter and, when foaming, place in the kidneys and mushrooms. Cook for 3 minutes on HIGH, in two batches. Melt the remaining butter in a casserole for 30 seconds on HIGH and add the onion. Cook for 1-2 minutes to soften slightly and stir in the flour. Gradually stir in the stock and sherry. Add the thyme and tomato paste, spoon in the kidneys and mushrooms, scraping the browning dish to remove the meat juices. Add a pinch of salt and pepper and cover the casserole. Cook on HIGH for 3 minutes. Stir well and cook a further 2 minutes on HIGH or until the kidneys are just tender. Stir in the cream and sprinkle with chopped parsley. Serve on, or surrounded by, triangles of hot, buttered toast, with the crusts removed.

Oeufs Florentine

PREPARATION TIME: 20 minutes

MICROWAVE COOKING TIME: 11½-13 minutes

SERVES: 4 people

1lb fresh spinach
4 eggs

SAUCE
4oz butter
Juice of ½ a lemon
Pinch cayenne pepper
Pinch dry mustard
2 egg yolks
Salt and pepper
Paprika

Wash the spinach well and remove any thick stalks. Place in a roasting bag and tie loosely with string. Cook on HIGH for 5-6 minutes, drain if necessary before using. To poach the eggs, pour 6 tbsps of hot water and a few drops of vinegar into each of 4 small dishes. Microwave on HIGH for about 1-2 minutes to bring to the boil. Break an egg into each dish and pierce the yolk with a skewer. Arrange the dishes in a circle and cook on HIGH for 2½-3 minutes.

This page: Oeufs Florentine. Facing page: Red Flannel Hash (top) and Sherried Kidneys and Mushrooms (bottom).

Alternatively, cook on MEDIUM for 3-3¼ minutes. Allow the eggs to stand in the water for 30 seconds-1 minute before removing. If preparing the eggs in advance, place cooked eggs in a dish of cold water and keep until needed. To prepare the sauce, place the butter in a large, glass measure and heat on HIGH for 1½-2 minutes. Mix the lemon juice with the cayenne pepper, mustard and egg yolks and beat into the hot butter. Beat well and then add salt and pepper to taste. Cook on MEDIUM for 1 minute. Whisk the sauce thoroughly after 15 seconds and then continue cooking for another 15 seconds. Do not allow the sauce to boil. If the sauce begins to curdle, dip the glass measure into a bowl of cold water to stop the cooking. Whisk well and continue cooking until the sauce thickens. Season the spinach with salt and pepper and some grated nutmeg, if desired. Divide the spinach between 4 serving dishes. Spread it out evenly, leaving a slight well in the center. Drain the poached eggs and place 1 egg in each dish. Cover the dishes and reheat on HIGH for 30 seconds. Pour over the sauce and serve immediately. To double the recipe, increase cooking time by half as much again.

Kedgeree

PREPARATION TIME: 25 minutes

MICROWAVE COOKING TIME: 27-32 minutes plus standing time

SERVES: 8 people

1lb smoked haddock or cod
1 cup long-grain rice
2 tsps oil
6oz cooked, peeled shrimp
2 hard-boiled eggs
1-2 tsps mild curry powder
¾ cup light cream
Chopped parsley
Nutmeg

Place the fish in a covered casserole and cook on HIGH for 10-12 minutes. Flake the fish and discard the skin and bones. Place the rice in a large, deep bowl with 2 cups boiling water, a pinch of salt and the oil. Cover with plastic wrap and cook on HIGH for 12 minutes, stirring halfway through to separate the grains. Leave to stand for 7 minutes. Drain if all the water has not been absorbed. Stir in the flaked fish and shrimp and leave covered. Place the curry powder and the cream in a glass measure or a small, deep bowl. Cook on HIGH for 3-5 minutes or until almost boiling. Chop 1 of the hard-boiled eggs and add it to the rice and fish with the cream. Stir gently and spoon into a serving dish. Garnish the top with the remaining hard-boiled egg sliced, chopped or cut into eighths. Sprinkle over chopped parsley and paprika before serving. If necessary, reheat the kedgeree for 2-3 minutes on HIGH before garnishing with the hard-boiled egg.

This page: Kedgeree. Facing page: Scones (top) and Shortbread (bottom).

TREATS FOR TEA

Shortbread

PREPARATION TIME: 15 minutes

MICROWAVE COOKING TIME: 4½-6 minutes

MAKES: 10

½ cup butter or margarine
4 tbsps sugar
1 cup all-purpose flour
4 tbsps rice flour
Pinch salt
4oz semi-sweet chocolate

Put the flour into a bowl with the rice flour and a pinch of salt. Rub in the butter or margarine until the mixture resembles fine breadcrumbs. Stir in half the sugar and knead the ingredients together lightly to form a dough. Line an 7 inch flan dish with wax paper. Alternatively, line the whole dish with plastic wrap. Press in the prepared shortbread mixture and smooth the top. Mark into 10 wedges and prick well with a fork. Cook on HIGH for 3-4 minutes. Sprinkle with the remaining sugar and allow to cool slightly. Cut through the markings in the wedges, remove from the dish and allow to cool on a wire rack. Melt the chocolate for 1½-2 minutes on MEDIUM, stirring until smooth. Holding the pointed end of each wedge of shortbread, place in the chocolate to coat about 2 inches or drizzle over the chocolate. Allow the chocolate to set and cool completely before serving.

Scones

PREPARATION TIME: 15 minutes

MICROWAVE COOKING TIME: 2-3½ minutes

MAKES: 9

1 cup whole-wheat flour
1½ tsps baking powder
Pinch salt
2 tbsps butter or margarine
½ cup golden raisins
6 tbsps milk

Sift the flour, baking powder and a pinch of salt into a mixing bowl. Return the bran to the bowl. Cut in the butter or margarine until the mixture resembles fine breadcrumbs. This may be done in a food processor or by hand. Stir in the golden raisins by hand and add the milk, gradually, until the dough comes together. It may not be necessary to add all the milk. Knead the dough lightly and turn it out onto a floured surface. Roll out to a thickness of ½-1 inch. Using a 2 inch round pastry cutter, cut the dough into approximately 9 rounds. The dough may also be cut into squares. Sprinkle each scone lightly with a mixture of sugar and cinnamon and place close together around the edge of a 9 inch round dish or microwave baking tray. Cook on HIGH for 2-3½ minutes or until the scones spring back lightly when touched. If necessary, rearrange the scones several times during cooking. Serve warm with jam and cream or butter.

Dundee Cake

PREPARATION TIME: 20 minutes

MICROWAVE COOKING TIME: 41-47 minutes plus standing time

MAKES: 1 cake

¾ cup butter or margarine
¾ cup dark brown sugar
3 eggs, lightly beaten
2 tbsps molasses
2 tbsps whiskey
2 cups all-purpose flour
1½ tbsps baking powder
1 tbsp allspice
½ cup chopped almonds
½ cup candied cherries, chopped
4½ cups mixed dried fruit (raisins, golden raisins, currants, candied peel)

DECORATION
Apricot jam
Blanched halved almonds
Candied cherries, halved

Soften the butter or margarine in a large bowl for 10-20 seconds on HIGH. Gradually beat in the sugar until light and fluffy. Beat in the eggs, one at a time, and add the molasses and whiskey. Beat until smooth and then sift in the flour, baking powder and spice. Carefully fold into the cream mixture and add the fruit, nuts and cherries. Use a 7 inch straight-sided deep baking dish, lightly greased and lined with wax paper. Spoon the prepared cake mixture into the dish and cook on LOW or DEFROST for 40-45 minutes. Leave to stand for 5 minutes before removing from the dish to cool on a wire rack. Melt the apricot jam for 1-2 minutes on HIGH, stir and sieve. Brush a thin layer of jam over the top of the cake while it is still warm and decorate with the almond and candied cherries before the jam sets completely. Leave to cool completely before serving.

Orange Cake

PREPARATION TIME: 25 minutes

MICROWAVE COOKING TIME: 7½ minutes plus standing time

MAKES: 1 cake

¾ cup butter or margarine
¾ cup sugar
3 eggs
Grated rind of 2 oranges
1½ cups all-purpose flour
2 tsps baking powder
Orange juice or milk

ORANGE FROSTING
2 cups sifted powdered sugar
Juice of 1 orange made up to 4-5 tbsps with water
Rind of 1 orange cut into thin strips

Lightly grease the base and sides of a 7 inch diameter deep cake dish. Line the base with a circle of wax paper. Soften the butter or margarine for 30 seconds on HIGH in a large bowl. Mix in the sugar and, when light and fluffy, gradually beat in the eggs. Add the grated rind while beating in the eggs. Sift the flour and the baking powder together and fold into the mixture. Add enough orange juice or milk to bring the mixture to a thick dropping consistency. Spoon the mixture into the prepared dish and smooth down the top. Cook on HIGH for 6 minutes. Leave the cake to stand in its dish on a flat surface for 5 minutes and then loosen the sides. Turn the cake out onto a wire rack set over a tray. For the frosting, place the orange juice and water, if using, in a deep bowl with the strips of orange rind. Cook on HIGH for 1 minute to soften the orange rind and to heat the liquid. Sift in about ¾ of the powdered sugar and stir to mix. The frosting should coat the back of a spoon and slowly run off if it is thick enough. Add remaining sugar if necessary or thin down with more hot water. When the cake is completely cool, pour the frosting onto the top and ease down the sides with a spatula. Allow to set completely before serving.

Apricot Nut Loaf

PREPARATION TIME: 20 minutes

MICROWAVE COOKING TIME: 4-5 minutes

MAKES: 1 loaf

4oz dried apricots, chopped
½ cup water
5 tbsps margarine
5 tbsps light brown sugar
1 cup all-purpose flour
1½ tsps baking powder
¼ tsp mixed spice or ground allspice
¼ tsp cinnamon
1 egg, slightly beaten
2 tsps golden syrup
3 tbsps milk
½ cup chopped almonds or walnuts

Combine the apricots and water in a small bowl and cover loosely. Heat on HIGH for 2 minutes and leave to stand for 30 minutes. Combine the remaining ingredients except the nuts and mix well. Drain the apricots and reserve the juice. Stir the nuts and apricots into the loaf mixture, adding enough of the reserved apricot juice to bring to a soft dropping

Facing page: Dundee Cake.

consistency. Line a loaf dish with wax paper and spoon in the loaf mixture. Microwave on HIGH for 4 minutes. Reduce the setting to LOW and continue cooking for 8-9 minutes. Stand for 5 minutes before removing from the dish. When cool, sprinkle the top with powdered sugar.

Chocolate Walnut Layer Cake

PREPARATION TIME: 25 minutes

MICROWAVE COOKING TIME: 11½-14 minutes plus standing time

MAKES: 1 cake

CHOCOLATE CAKE

1 cup butter or margarine
1⅛ cups brown sugar
½ cup vegetable oil
4 eggs
1½ cups all-purpose flour
2 tsps baking powder
4 tbsps cocoa

FILLING

3 tbsps butter or margarine
½ cup walnuts, finely chopped
2 tbsps light cream or evaporated milk
2 cups powdered sugar
½ tsp rum extract

TOPPING

4oz semi-sweet chocolate
Walnut halves
Powdered sugar

Line a 7 inch microwave cake dish with plastic wrap or place a wax paper circle in the bottom of a greased dish. Place the butter or margarine in a deep bowl and microwave on HIGH for 10-20 seconds to soften. Using an electric mixer, add the sugar and the oil gradually, making sure the sugar is well blended and the mixture is light and fluffy. When the sugar is no longer grainy, gradually beat in the eggs. If the mixture begins to curdle, add a little flour and whisk again. Put the remaining flour with the baking powder and cocoa and fold into the cream mixture. Pour the mixture into the baking dish and cook on HIGH for 7 minutes. Leave to cool on a flat surface in the dish for 5-10 minutes and then remove to a cooling rack. While the cake cools, prepare the filling. Microwave the butter or margarine in a small mixing bowl on HIGH for about 1 minute or until melted. Stir in the walnuts and heat a further 2-4 minutes on HIGH until the butter and the nuts are light brown. Stir every 2 minutes. Sift in the powdered sugar and beat well. Gradually add the cream until the filling is of spreading consistency. Add the rum extract and set aside. Cut the cake horizontally into 3 layers and sandwich with the walnut filling. Break up the chocolate for the topping and put it into a small bowl. Microwave on MEDIUM for 1½-2 minutes, stirring often until the chocolate is spreadable. Using a spatula, spread the chocolate onto the top of the cake. Toss the walnuts into the powdered sugar to coat lightly. Shake off the excess sugar and, when the chocolate topping is nearly set, arrange the walnuts around the outside edge of the cake. Allow the chocolate to set completely before cutting to serve.

This page: Apricot Nut Loaf (top) and Orange Cake (bottom). Facing page: Chocolate Walnut Layer Cake.

menier
menier
menier
menier

COCKTAIL SAVORIES

Shrimp on Horseback

PREPARATION TIME: 30 minutes

MICROWAVE COOKING TIME: 7-8 minutes

MAKES: 16

8 slices bacon, rinds and bones removed
16 large uncooked shrimp, peeled but tail ends left on
1 large green pepper, seeded and cut into 16 even-sized pieces
16 anchovy fillets, soaked in 4 tbsps milk
4 tbsps lemon juice
Dash tabasco
16 whole chives (optional)

Precook the bacon on a microwave roasting rack or on a plate with paper towels. Place two layers of paper towels on a plate and arrange 4 slices of bacon on the towel; cover with another sheet of paper towel. Arrange another 4 slices on top and cover with another towel. If using a microwave roasting rack place the strips of bacon in an even layer. Cook on HIGH for 4 minutes, or until the bacon is slightly brown but not completely cooked. Meanwhile, drain the anchovies, rinse in cold water and pat dry. Place a shrimp on top of each slice of pepper and wrap an anchovy around the middle. Sprinkle with lemon juice and a dash of tabasco. Cut the bacon strips in half and wrap one half around each shrimp. If using chives, soften for 15 seconds on HIGH in a small dish of water. Drain and tie up each shrimp roll. Alternatively, secure with wooden picks. Place the shrimp on a plate or in a microwave baking dish. Cook on HIGH for 3-4 minutes or until the shrimp are cooked.

Sweet and Sour Sausages

PREPARATION TIME: 25 minutes

MICROWAVE COOKING TIME: 6-10 minutes plus standing time

SERVES: 6-8 people

1lb pork sausages
2 tbsps oil
8oz canned pineapple pieces, drained and juice reserved
1 large or 2 small green peppers, seeded and cut into 1 inch pieces
8oz cherry tomatoes (if unavailable, substitute 1 large or 2 small sweet red peppers, seeded and cut into 1 inch pieces)

SAUCE
1 tbsp cornstarch
2 tbsps brown sugar
¼ tsp ground ginger
1 clove garlic, crushed
1 tbsp tomato ketchup
1 tbsp soy sauce
Reserved pineapple juice

Heat a browning dish according to the manufacturer's directions. Prick the sausage skins all over with a fork. When the browning dish is hot, add the oil and the sausages and cook for 3 minutes on HIGH, turning frequently to brown evenly. Drain the sausages on paper towels and cut them into 1 inch pieces. Combine all the sauce ingredients, stirring in the reserved pineapple juice gradually. Combine the sauce with all the other ingredients, except tomatoes, in a casserole dish and cook on HIGH for 3-7 minutes or until the sauce is thickened, stirring carefully two or three times. Add tomatoes and leave to stand 1-2 minutes. Provide wooden picks for serving.

Chicken Satays with Peppers

PREPARATION TIME: 25 minutes plus marinating time

MICROWAVE COOKING TIME: 11-15 minutes

SERVES: 6-8 people

4 chicken breasts, skinned and boned
3 small peppers, red, green and yellow

MARINADE
4 tbsps oil
Grated rind and juice of 1 lime
1 tsp dry mustard powder
1 tbsp light soy sauce
1 clove garlic, crushed

BASTING SAUCE
1 shallot, finely chopped
1 clove garlic, crushed
1 tbsp tomato paste
½ chili pepper, finely chopped
4 tbsps chicken stock
1 tbsp soy sauce
2 tbsps smooth peanut butter

GARNISH
Lime wedges

Facing page: Sweet and Sour Sausages.

Cut the chicken breasts into 1 inch pieces. Seed the pepper and cut them into pieces the same size as the chicken. Thread three pieces of chicken and three pieces of pepper, alternating the colors, onto small wooden skewers. Place them in a shallow microwave ovenproof dish. Mix together the marinade ingredients and pour over the satays. Cover with plastic wrap and leave to stand for 2 hours or overnight in the refrigerator. Turn the satays often to coat them evenly. Place all the sauce ingredients in a blender or food processor and purée until smooth. Pour into a small bowl and cook on HIGH for 5-6 minutes, until boiling, stirring frequently. Heat a browning dish according to the manufacturer's directions and when hot place the satays on the dish, turning to lightly brown all sides. Cook in the browning dish or on a microwave oven rack for 5-7 minutes, turning frequently and basting with the sauce. Combine any remaining sauce with the remaining marinade and reheat on HIGH for 1-2 minutes. Before serving, brush the satays lightly with sauce and serve the remaining sauce separately.

This page: Shrimp on Horseback. Facing page: Chicken Satays with Peppers (top) and Lamb and Mint Meatballs (bottom).

Lamb and Mint Meatballs

PREPARATION TIME: 20 minutes

MICROWAVE COOKING TIME: 8 minutes

SERVES: 6-8 people

1lb ground lamb
1 medium onion, roughly chopped
¼ tsp ground allspice
Salt and pepper
2 tsps chopped fresh mint
2 tsps chopped fresh parsley
4 slices bread, crusts removed
Water
Fresh mint leaves, as large as possible

GARNISH
Lemon twists

Chop the onion in a food processor until fine. Add the lamb, allspice, salt, pepper, chopped mint, chopped parsley and the bread slices, torn into small pieces. Process again to mix, but do not overwork the meat. Add about 4 tbsps water and process again briefly. The mixture should be very moist but still hold together. Use more water if necessary. Pat the mixture into 1 inch balls. Wrap each meatball in a mint leaf. Place the meatballs on a microwave baking sheet or in a shallow dish. Place the ends of the mint leaves on the bottom. Cook on HIGH for 5 minutes. Turn over and reposition the meatballs and cook a further 3 minutes on HIGH or until fully cooked. Garnish serving dish with lemon twists.

Hot Salmon and Horseradish Pinwheels

PREPARATION TIME: 25 minutes

MICROWAVE COOKING TIME: 1-2 minutes 20 seconds

SERVES: 6-8 people

8oz smoked salmon, thinly sliced
8oz cream, curd or low fat soft cheese
1 tbsp prepared horseradish sauce
2 tsps chopped fresh or dried dill
1 medium-sized cucumber, cut into

½ inch thick rounds

Place slices of smoked salmon on separate sheets of plastic wrap. Soften the cheese for 20 seconds on HIGH and mix with the horseradish and dill. Divide the cheese mixture among all the slices of smoked salmon and spread evenly. Roll-up the salmon jelly roll fashion and wrap tightly in the plastic wrap. Place in the freezer until well chilled and firm, but not frozen. Score the skin of the cucumber, lengthwise, with the prongs of a fork, if desired. Slice the cucumber and sprinkle lightly with salt. Leave to drain on paper towels for 30 minutes. Rinse well and pat dry. Slice the salmon rolls crosswise into ¼ inch slices. Place one slice on each slice of cucumber and arrange in a circle on a plate or microwave baking sheet. Heat for 1-2 minutes on HIGH before serving.

This page: Hot Salmon and Horseradish Pinwheels. Facing page: Pâté en Gelée.

BUFFET

Pâte en Gelée

PREPARATION TIME: 25 minutes plus chilling time

MICROWAVE COOKING TIME: 27-30 minutes

SERVES: 8-10 people

8oz rindless streaky bacon
1lb coarsely ground pork
8oz ground veal
8oz pork liver, skinned
1 clove garlic, crushed
¼ tsp ground allspice
2 tbsps aspic powder
¼ tsp ground nutmeg
¼ tsp ground ginger
2 cups water and white wine mixed half and half
½ tsp thyme
1 tsp chopped parsley
Salt and pepper
½ cup heavy cream
2 tbsps brandy
5oz thick-cut gammon or ham
2 bay leaves

DECORATION
Fresh herbs
Capers
Green peppercorns

Stretch the bacon with the back of a knife and use it to line a 6 cup glass loaf dish. Combine the ground meats, liver, garlic, spices, herbs, salt and pepper in a food processor and work to chop roughly. Add the cream and the brandy and process once or twice to mix. Cut the ham or gammon into strips and set aside. Place ⅓ of the meat mixture into the lined terrine and spread smoothly. Place a layer of ham or gammon on top and then cover with a layer of meat. Repeat with the remaining gammon and meat mixture, smooth down the top and fold any overlapping strips of bacon. Place 2 bay leaves on the top and cover the dish with plastic wrap. Cook on MEDIUM for 12 minutes. Allow the pâté to rest for 5 minutes. Cook on MEDIUM for a further 20 minutes. Cover the top of the pâté with foil and weight down. Chill for at least 2-4 hours or overnight. To serve, prepare aspic as for the Salmon in Aspic. Slice the pâté in ¼ inch slices and place them on a cooling rack. Decorate the slices with small sprigs of fresh herbs, capers, green peppercorns or pimento. Pour a small amount of nearly set aspic over the top of the decoration to set it. When the aspic is completely set, coat the whole slice of pâté with a thin layer of nearly set aspic. Allow to set and then arrange on a serving plate slightly overlapping. Put any remaining aspic in a tray, turn out when set and cut into cubes or chop roughly. Pile the aspic in the middle of the pâté slices to serve.

Salmon in Aspic

PREPARATION TIME: 35 minutes

MICROWAVE COOKING TIME: 32-39 minutes

SERVES: 8-10 people

3¼ lbs whole salmon or salmon trout
Whole dill or fennel
Oil for brushing
2 tbsps aspic powder
2 cups water and white wine mixed half and half
Fresh herbs for decoration
Pimento
Lemon or lime slices
Fresh bay leaves

Rinse the salmon and dry well. Trim off the fins and brush the skin lightly with oil. Place dill or fennel inside the fish for extra flavor. Cover the head and tail with foil and cover the foil with a double thickness of plastic wrap. Make a steam hole with a sharp knife on either side of the dorsal fin. Curve the fish to fit the turntable and then loosely tie the head to the tail with a slip knot. Cook on LOW or DEFROST for 26-29 minutes. Remove the string, plastic wrap and foil halfway through cooking time. To test if the salmon is cooked, insert a sharp knife into one of the steam holes at the dorsal fin. The blade should pass easily through the fish if it is fully cooked. Allow the fish to cool slightly and then peel away the skin using a filleting knife or a table knife. Cover the fish loosely with plastic wrap and allow to cool completely. Remove the herbs from inside the fish and discard them. Place the fish on a serving dish while preparing the aspic and decorations. Bring the water and wine to the boil in a deep bowl or glass measure. This should take about 4-6 minutes. Stir in the aspic powder and heat 1-2 minutes on HIGH to dissolve it completely. Place the bowl or glass measure into a bowl of iced water and allow the aspic to cool completely, until almost set. Brush a thin layer of the aspic over the salmon and allow it to set. To re-use the aspic, melt 1-2 minutes on HIGH and stir gently. Allow to thicken slightly again in iced water and spoon a thin layer over the salmon. When almost set, decorate with small sprigs of fresh herbs, lemon slices, bay leaves and pimento. Reheat the aspic once more and thicken it again over ice. Carefully spoon the thickened aspic over the decorations and leave to set completely. Pour the remaining aspic into a shallow pan and set in the refrigerator. Remove the set aspic and turn out onto a dampened cutting board. Cut into small cubes or chop roughly. Use to decorate serving dish for the salmon along with small bunches of fresh herbs and lemon slices.

Salad Singapore

PREPARATION TIME: 25 minutes plus marinating time

MICROWAVE COOKING TIME: 10-15 minutes

SERVES: 6-8 people

1 3¼ lb chicken
1 tsp freshly ground black pepper
1 tsp ground mustard
1 tsp ground ginger
1 clove garlic, crushed
½ tsp ground turmeric
1 tsp mild curry powder
2 tbsps vegetable oil
4 tbsps raw peanuts
8oz zucchini, sliced diagonally
1 red pepper, seeded and shredded
8oz pea pods
1 medium-sized cucumber
2 tbsps desiccated coconut

Skin and bone the chicken and cut the meat into shreds. Mix all the spices together and toss with the chicken. Allow to stand in the refrigerator for at least 2 hours. Heat a browning dish according to the manufacturer's directions and add the oil. Add the peanuts and cook on HIGH for 2-3 minutes, stirring frequently until lightly browned. Remove the peanuts with a draining spoon and add the zucchini, red pepper and pea pods to the browning dish. Return to the microwave oven and cook on HIGH for 2 minutes. Place in a serving dish and keep warm. If necessary, add another 1 tbsp oil to the browning dish and reheat. Add the chicken and cook in small batches for 5-7 minutes on HIGH. Cut the cucumber into thin strips and add to the vegetables in the serving dish. Add the chicken and the peanuts and toss thoroughly. Sprinkle over the desiccated coconut and reheat for 1-2 minutes on HIGH if desired before serving. May also be served cold.

Potato, Cucumber and Dill Salad

PREPARATION TIME: 20 minutes

MICROWAVE COOKING TIME: 16-22 minutes

SERVES: 6-8 people

1lb even-sized small new potatoes, scrubbed
3 sprigs dill
Salt
1 cucumber, cut into 1 inch chunks

DRESSING
1 whole egg and 1 egg yolk
½ pint oil
2 tbsps chopped fresh dill or 1 tbsp dried dill
1 tbsp mild mustard
1 tbsp white wine vinegar
1 green onion, finely chopped

GARNISH
Sprigs of fresh dill

Facing page: Salmon in Aspic.

Put the potatoes into a large bowl with the dill and salt. Pour over enough boiling water to cover. Cover the bowl with pierced plastic wrap and cook on HIGH for 15-20 minutes or until the potatoes are tender. Do not allow the potatoes to boil too rapidly. Reduce the setting to MEDIUM if necessary. Drain and leave the potatoes to cool. Prepare the dressing in a food processor. Combine the eggs with all the remaining ingredients except the oil. With the machine running, gradually pour the oil through the feed tube in a thin, steady stream. Add salt and pepper to taste. Place the chunks of cucumber in a casserole with 4 tbsps water. Cook on HIGH for 1-2 minutes to blanch. Rinse immediately under cold water and leave to dry. Combine the potatoes and the cucumbers in a bowl with the dressing. Transfer to a serving dish and garnish with sprigs of fresh dill.

This page: Boeuf Niçoise. Facing page: Cheesecake (top) and Chocolate Truffle Cake (bottom).

Chocolate Truffle Cake

PREPARATION TIME: 20 minutes

MICROWAVE COOKING TIME: 7 minutes

SERVES: 8-10 people

12oz semi-sweet chocolate
½ cup butter
4 tbsps brandy or rum
2 eggs
2 cups graham crackers, crushed
½ cup chopped blanched almonds
1 cup whipped cream
Chocolate curls

Melt the chocolate and butter together on MEDIUM for 5 minutes. Beat in the eggs and heat a further 2 minutes on MEDIUM, stirring twice to thicken the eggs. Stir in the brandy, biscuits and chopped almonds. Spread into a 7 inch springform or removable base pan. Chill overnight until firm. Transfer to a serving dish and pile the cream on top. Decorate the top with chocolate curls. To prepare chocolate curls, take a thick block of semi-sweet chocolate and microwave on MEDIUM LOW for 30-60 seconds or until the chocolate is just barely warm. Turn the chocolate once or twice while heating. To form the curls, draw a swivel vegetable peeler towards you across the edge of the chocolate in a continuous, even motion. Chocolate curls may be kept in an airtight container.

Cheesecake

PREPARATION TIME: 30 minutes

MICROWAVE COOKING TIME: 14-25½ minutes

SERVES: 6-8 people

FILLING
1lb cream cheese
⅔ cup sugar
Pinch salt
⅓ cup light cream
Rind and juice of ½ lemon
Pinch ground coriander
4 eggs

CRUST
4 tbsps butter or margarine
¾ cup graham crackers, crushed
2 tbsps sugar

TOPPING
1 kiwi fruit, peeled and thinly sliced
2-3 satsumas, pith carefully removed
4oz fresh strawberries, washed and halved or raspberries (if strawberries or raspberries are unavailable, use purple grapes, halved and seeded)
Green seedless grapes, halved
Apricot jam

Place the cream cheese in a bowl and microwave on MEDIUM for 1 minute or until softened. Beat in the sugar, salt, cream and lemon rind. Gradually blend in the lemon juice and eggs. Cook on HIGH for 4-7 minutes, stirring very well every 2 minutes. Line the bottom of a 9 inch round baking dish with a circle of wax paper. Pour in the cream cheese mixture and cook on MEDIUM for 7-15 minutes or until almost set. Meanwhile prepare the crust. Mix the crushed graham crackers in a food processor or blender with the sugar. Work until fine. Melt the butter for 1½-2 minutes on HIGH. With the machine running, pour in the butter to mix with the crumbs. When the cheese filling is nearly set, carefully spoon over the crumb crust. Press down lightly and cook on HIGH for 1½ minutes. Allow the cheesecake to cool in the dish and then refrigerate overnight. To decorate, loosen the cheesecake from the sides of the dish and turn out onto a serving plate. Carefully peel away the disc of paper from the top. Arrange the various prepared fruits in circles on top of the cheesecake. Melt the apricot jam for 1 minute on HIGH and strain. Brush the fruit with a light layer of warm glaze, making sure that all the fruit is covered completely. Allow the glaze to set before serving.

Boeuf Niçoise

PREPARATION TIME: 30 minutes plus chilling time

MICROWAVE COOKING TIME: 23-31 minutes

SERVES: 8-10 people

1lb beef tenderloin

SALAD
1 head cauliflower, trimmed into flowerets
8oz broccoli, trimmed into flowerets
8oz green beans, trimmed
8 tomatoes, peeled and quartered
½ cup black olives, stoned

DRESSING
4oz olive oil
2 tbsps white wine vinegar
2 tsps Dijon mustard
2 tsps chopped fresh basil
1 tsp chopped fresh parsley
Salt and pepper

Place the meat on a microwave roasting rack with the thinner portion of the meat tucked under for an even shape. Tie with string to keep the shape. Wrap the ends of the beef with foil, shiny side down, and cook on HIGH for 3 minutes. Remove the foil from the beef and reduce the power to MEDIUM. Cook a further 5-8 minutes longer, turning the beef over once. Allow to stand until cool. The meat should be rare. If desired, brush the beef lightly with gravy browning before beginning to cook. Bring 4 cups water to the boil in a large glass bowl for 8-11 minutes on HIGH. Drop in 4 tomatoes and leave for 5 seconds. Remove to a bowl of iced water and reboil the water. Repeat with a further 4 tomatoes. Skin the tomatoes, quarter them and set them aside. Place the cauliflower flowerets in a casserole dish with 4 tbsps water and a pinch of salt. Cover the dish and cook on HIGH for 4-5 minutes. Place the broccoli flowerets in the water after 2 minutes of cooking time. Drain the vegetables and rinse under cold water to stop the cooking. Cook the beans in a casserole dish with 6 tbsps water. Cover the dish and cook on HIGH for 3-4 minutes. Rinse the beans under cold water to stop the cooking and leave them to drain with the cauliflower and the broccoli. Mix the dressing ingredients together in a large bowl and when the vegetables are dry add them to the dressing along with the tomatoes and the olives. Toss the vegetables to coat, then leave in the refrigerator for 1 hour to marinate. To assemble the salad, slice the beef thinly and arrange on a serving plate in a semi-circle with the slices overlapping. Using a draining spoon, pile the vegetable salad onto the plate. Pour some of the remaining dressing over the meat before serving.

This page: Salad Singapore (top) and Potato, Cucumber and Dill Salad (bottom). Facing page: Raspberry Ripple Cake.

A CHILDREN'S PARTY

Raspberry Ripple Cake

PREPARATION TIME: 2 minutes

MICROWAVE COOKING TIME: 11-13 minutes

MAKES: 1 cake

¾ cup butter or margarine
¾ cup sugar
3 eggs, lightly beaten
1½ cups all-purpose flour
Salt
2 tsps baking powder
3 tbsps seedless raspberry jam
2 tbsps hot water (optional)
Few drops red food coloring

FROSTING
3 tbsps seedless raspberry jam
4 cups powdered sugar
Hot water

Heat butter or margarine for 1 minute on HIGH to soften. Beat until creamy, and gradually beat in the sugar until light and fluffy. Gradually beat in the eggs until the mixture is mousse-like and all the eggs have been incorporated. Sift in the flour with a pinch of salt and the baking powder. Fold the dry ingredients into the butter, sugar and eggs. Divide the mixture into two bowls and add the raspberry jam and red food coloring to half the mixture. Stir thoroughly. Add hot water to the plain half as necessary to bring the mixture to soft dropping consistency. Line a round or decorative microwave cake dish with plastic wrap. Fill with spoonfuls of the two mixtures, alternating the colors. Draw a knife or spatula through the mixtures to marble the two colors. Cook for 6-8 minutes on HIGH, turning the dish occasionally if it is not a round shape. If the corners of the cake appear to be overcooking, cover with foil if your oven manufacturer allows its use. Leave in the dish for 5 minutes before turning out to cool. Soften the jam for the frosting for 20 seconds on HIGH and beat until smooth. Fill a pastry bag fitted with a small writing tube with the jam. Heat about 1 cup water on HIGH for 4-5 minutes. Sift in the powdered sugar gradually, beating until the frosting coats the back of a spoon but runs off slowly. It may not be necessary to add all the sugar. Pour over the cake, using a spatula to help spread the frosting. Pipe thin lines of jam over the cake before the frosting

sets completely. Quickly swirl the jam through the frosting with a skewer and allow to set completely before cutting to serve.

Chocolate Marshmallow Turtles

PREPARATION TIME: 15 minutes

MICROWAVE COOKING TIME: 2 minutes 15 seconds-4½ minutes

MAKES: 12

48 shelled pecans
12 marshmallows
½ cup chocolate chips
1 tbsp vegetable shortening

Put the pecans in groups of 4 on a microwave baking sheet lined with nonstick paper. Place a marshmallow on top of the pecans. Microwave on HIGH for 15-30 seconds or until the marshmallows just start to puff. Place the chocolate chips and the vegetable shortening in a small bowl. Microwave on MEDIUM for 2-4 minutes, stirring frequently until the chocolate melts. Spoon over the top of each turtle to cover the marshmallow. Leave to set completely before serving.

Chocolate Squares

PREPARATION TIME: 30 minutes

MICROWAVE COOKING TIME: 5 minutes

MAKES: 16

4 tbsps butter or margarine
6oz semi-sweet chocolate
2 tbsps golden syrup or honey
2 cups graham crackers, crushed
Colored candied cherries

Place the butter or margarine, chocolate and syrup or honey in a small, deep bowl and heat on MEDIUM for 5 minutes, stirring occasionally until the chocolate melts. Stir in the biscuit crumbs and mix thoroughly. Grease a shallow 7 inch square pan and spoon in the chocolate mixture. Smooth the top and mark into squares with a sharp knife. Cut the candied cherries in half and put a half on top of each square, alternating the colors. Leave to set completely and then cut into squares to serve.

Granola Bars

PREPARATION TIME: 15 minutes

MICROWAVE COOKING TIME: 7-8 minutes

MAKES: 12

6 cups toasted fruit and nut granola
½ cup butter or margarine
½ cup dark brown sugar
Pinch salt
2 eggs, beaten
Few drops vanilla extract

Place the butter or margarine in a glass measure and microwave for 45 seconds-1 minute on HIGH. Combine the brown sugar, salt, eggs and flavoring in a large bowl and gradually beat in the melted butter. Add the granola and stir to coat well. Lightly grease a 12 x 8 inch baking dish and press in the mixture. Cook on HIGH for 6-8 minutes or until just firm to the touch. If the corners of the mixture seem to be cooking before the center, place foil across all 4 corners and continue cooking. Press the mixture with a spatula every few minutes to smooth down. Before allowing to cool, cut the mixture into 12 bars. Allow to cool

completely before removing from the dish.

Animal Crackers

PREPARATION TIME: 20 minutes

MICROWAVE COOKING TIME: 2-4 minutes

MAKES: 24

1 cup all-purpose flour
½ cup whole-wheat flour
2 tbsps sugar
½ tsp bicarbonate of soda
¼ tsp salt
¼ tsp ground cinnamon
4 tbsps vegetable shortening
1 tbsp butter or margarine
2 tbsps water
1 tbsp honey
1 tbsp molasses
Few drops vanilla extract

Sift the flours with the sugar, bicarbonate of soda, salt and cinnamon into a deep bowl. Return the bran to the bowl. Cut in the vegetable shortening and butter or margarine until the particles are the size of small peas. This may also be done in a food processor. Combine the water, honey, molasses and vanilla in a small bowl. Mix with the dry ingredients, tossing and mashing with a fork until the particles cling together. Form into a ball, cover with plastic wrap and refrigerate at least 1 hour. Divide the dough in half and roll out to ¼ inch thickness on a well-floured surface. Flour the rolling pin frequently while rolling out. Cut the dough with animal shaped cookie cutters. Prick lightly with a fork and transfer to a plate or microwave baking sheet lined with wax paper. Cook 12 cookies at a time arranged in a circle around the edge of the plate or baking sheet. Cook on HIGH for 1-2 minutes or until the surface of the dough is dry and firm to touch. Cool on a wire rack. Sprinkle lightly with powdered sugar or decorate with melted chocolate or colored frostings.

Facing page: Animal Crackers (top) and Chocolate Marshmallow Turtles (bottom). This page: Granola Bars (top) and Chocolate Squares (bottom).

INDEX

Dep. Leg. B-32314-87